# This Rough Magic

# THIS ROUGH MAGIC
## The Life of Teaching

### DANIEL A. LINDLEY

**BERGIN & GARVEY**
Westport, Connecticut • London

**Library of Congress Cataloging-in-Publication Data**

Lindley, Daniel A.
    This rough magic : the life of teaching / Daniel A. Lindley.
        p. cm.
    Includes bibliographical references (p. ) and index.
    ISBN 0–89789–363–8.—ISBN 0–89789–366–2 (pbk.)
      1. Teachers—United States. 2. Teaching. I. Title.
    LB1775.2.L56  1993
    371.1'02—dc20       93–25009

British Library Cataloguing in Publication Data is available.

Library of Congress Catalog Card Number: 93–25009
ISBN: 0–89789–363–8
     0–89789–366–2 (pbk.)

First published in 1993

Bergin & Garvey, 88 Post Road West, Westport, CT 06881
An imprint of Greenwood Publishing Group, Inc.

Printed in the United States of America

∞™

The paper used in this book complies with the
Permanent Paper Standard issued by the National
Information Standards Organization (Z39.48–1984).

10 9 8 7 6 5 4 3 2 1

## Copyright Acknowledgments

This book is for the guides, mentors, teachers who were
with me, and move me still:

| | |
|---|---|
| Ludlow Baldwin | Jerome Bruner |
| Frank Trevor | William Rogge |
| René Clark | James McCrimmon |
| William Madsen | Dwight Burton |
| John Bayley | Nancy Thompson |
| Sally Barrett | Lucia Woods |
| Cleanth Brooks | Garey Malek |

*You have dressed the unknowable in the garments of the known.*

—Djuna Barnes, *Nightwood*, 193

# Contents

# Preface

Schooling, one way or another, has happened to all of us. So a book about teaching is inevitably permeated by memories. These are, of course, memories of actual schools, the air mixed with chalk dust and the aromas of floor wax and cafeteria kitchens and the sound of crowds of students in hallways or on the playground. For twelve years we were taught, scheduled, let out for recess or vacations, and brought back again, to school. And it must be admitted at the outset that much of what actually happened in school has turned out to be of little significance. Most of our teachers have faded into hazy memory, and most of what they taught us has just disappeared, perhaps leaving only a faint cloud of guilt: We *should* remember how to conjugate the past tense of "avoir," or how to solve a quadratic equation . . . but much of that is gone.

This book is about what is *not* gone. It is about those teachers who have stayed with us, vivid figures who made a difference. It is an inquiry into why they have done so: what they did, and why. It is about what moved them to move us. In short, it is a book about success, and success in one of life's hardest tasks.

Such success is relatively rare. For many years I have asked my students in teacher education programs how many teachers they remember, with real affection or respect, from their secondary schools, grades seven through twelve. In American schools they will have had, over that time, thirty teachers, more or less. But the ones they remember favorably are few indeed, usually only two or three. And these students are people who have elected to teach. Clearly they hope to do better than almost all of the teachers they had. But, equally clearly, the odds are against them. By tracing the outlines of the life of teaching, I hope to lower those odds, for both new and experienced teachers. I am interested in what happens in actual successful classrooms, but I am just as interested in what happens in the psyche of the successful teacher over time. Technique without the involvement of the teacher's soul—psyche, literally—is worse than hollow: It is a sham, and will immediately be seen through by students. But students are equally adept at recognizing the coming together of teaching and teacher. Students have a sure sense of authenticity.

To explore psyche has meant, for me, an exploration of my own life in teaching, and some of that has perforce found its way into this book. When they were younger, my two children, Dan and Helen, tolerated my lectures over breakfast, if not the quiz at dinner. Later, Helen and I went through graduate programs in social work at the same time; it was illuminating and helpful for me to share my student status with her. And I have long been my son's pupil: He has taught me how to make my computer do things beyond all my imagining. (Sometimes, wisely, he has skipped me and taught my computer directly.)

In exploring my life in teaching I have tried to pick only experiences that are common to the learning of teaching generally. Thus other teachers will recognize my hesitant beginnings and, I hope, my gradual growth of confidence. They will recognize in my students some of theirs, because adolescents are pretty much the same everywhere. But I have left out of my account most of the particular people who taught me and who have stayed memorable, who matter as much to me now as they did when they first came into my life. These are the people to whom this book is dedicated. Three of them were classroom teachers of mine in high school; others taught me in college or graduate schools; still others clothed their teaching in friendship, or love. All have been my companions on the way; they have moved me along, and I am grateful beyond any words. I acknowledge my debt to them with this book. I treasure these people. They have given me more than they, and I, know. So have my students.

I have been fortunate in another way, too: I have not only had a life of teaching, but I have been given an opportunity to reflect on that life. Full-time teaching doesn't allow much time for reflection, but when I began my own analysis (in 1982) and then entered the Analyst Training Program of the C. G. Jung Institute in Chicago (in 1984) I was, in effect, *made* to reflect. This book is a result of that reflection. And it is not just that without the Jungian work there would have been a different book. There would have been no book at all. I spent lots of time wondering about teaching during the years I did it full-time, but the analyst training program gave me a way of wondering, and a theory to inform all that had gone before. For this too I am grateful; indeed, I am still a bit in awe of my good fortune.

# This Rough Magic

*Chapter One*

# Calling Spirits: The Art and the Life of Teaching

| | |
|---|---|
| *Ferdinand*: | This is a most majestic vision, and |
| | Harmonious charmingly. May I be bold |
| | To think these spirits? |
| *Prospero*: | Spirits, which by mine art |
| | I have from their confines called to enact |
| | My present fancies. |

—*The Tempest*, Act 4, Scene 1

A hundred and eighty days a year— every day of school—teachers, by their art, call spirits to enact their present fancies in their classrooms. This is a book about those spirits. They are of two kinds. There are "visible" spirits, the ones that are generated by knowledge and training. These come clothed as certification requirements, classroom management skills, curriculum design, tests, standards, scheduling: the whole public face of teaching. Then there are "invisible" spirits, such as the spirit that moved us to become teachers in the first place; or the one that governs our feelings as we stand in front of our class; or the one that doles out good days and bad days; or the one that more profoundly measures out elation and despair, memory and desire, childhood and adolescence, youth and age, in us and in our students. This book is about these two kinds of spirits and how they weave the pattern of our teaching lives.

Teaching is an unimaginably complex activity. In junior and senior high schools, a teacher typically will have five classes with anywhere between twenty and thirty students, each day, five days a week. Consider for a moment the experience of one student, as she records it in this poem:

### SCHOOL ANNOUNCEMENTS

Good morning, these are the school announcements . . .
   Did you hear what happened in Student Congress this
   morning? I hear they almost kicked the president
    out.
You put a curse on my locker and now it won't open!
The speed of a body falling is directly proportional to the
length of time that it falls when conditions are perfect.
   Buster wrote me that he has been sky-diving again.
Any other questions?
   Don't you love me any more? No.
   Ah . . .
On page 47 there is a problem worked for you at the top of
the page; you may study this example if you want to do well
on the test.
   Will somebody please tell me what the hell good are
   parabolas?
   What's black and white and black and white?
   Are you going to the dance tonight? The blacks are
   planning some kind of trouble.
What does Hamlet mean when he says "To be or not to be"?
A nun rolling down a hill?
You have two days to complete the worksheet for a grade.
Your history teacher did *what* last Saturday night? . . .
   . . . the National Honor Society will meet at 8:00
   tomorrow. . . .
   Do they bite?
Jim, do you have this memorized? Then why aren't
   you listening?
If pressure goes up, volume goes down. If temperature goes
   up, volume goes up.
   I thought you all broke up last week.

I just don't understand. What do you people have
    against learning?
Then she said he was crazy and just threw his ring back.
I used to understand it when Mrs. Fry taught it.
. . . tryouts for the school play will be at 8:00 today. . . .
Simply memorize the formulas for the test and then
don't worry about it.
    Find the equations of the axis of symmetry.
    I wish I could, but I have something to do now.
What did you get on number 8?
You can't do it that way because the book says this is
the only way it can be done.
    Shelley? Who's she?
Did they call off the French Club party?
    Some of you people have just missed the boat.
Attention all Seniors who have not had their pictures
taken—you need to make an appointment today. . . .
    Have you read *Rosemary's Baby*?
After all, I said to her, math isn't the only subject I
    take.
Who won the boat race in Chapter V?
Write me a note in 4th hour, OK?
. . . These have been the school announcements, have a good
    day. . . .

*  *  *  *

What happened at school today, dear?
Nothing, Mother.
    —Brenda Case, Eisenhower High School, Lawton, Oklahoma

As this poem makes wonderfully clear, we must think of teaching as happening on two planes at once, public and private, and in two domains, that of the teacher and that of each separate student. Publicly, teaching is what teachers "do," and what taxpayers pay them to do: They instruct, and therefore students are instructed. But privately teachers and students alike are subject to waves of often conflicting emotions and anxieties. Both must think of what they are about even as they remain ever vigilant for the unexpected adolescent disruption. Some teachers find pleasure in resonating with the inner world of the students in front of them, others are repelled by it. And the same is true for students: Some will be "with" the teacher, others opposed; some will daydream, some will sleep outright, some will be defiant either overtly or secretly (daydreaming is a form of defiance, surely). The complexity of teaching becomes immediately apparent if we imagine for a moment that we can tune in to the flow of thoughts and feelings and images contained in the teacher and in each of those twenty or thirty students and know, for each person, the full range of his or her inner life at every moment as the class proceeds. This entire range is the reality of teaching. To understand what teaching is, we must look not only at what is taught and how it is taught, but at what we cannot see, but must intuit.

Thus in order to understand teaching the classroom must be observed, and the observing must be informed by ideas, memories, and theory: specifically, an idea of method, together with an idea of how people connect with one another, how their stories overlap and resonate, how memory and desire and hope and fear combine in the flow of teaching. This book is an effort to observe teaching in this deep way. "Observe" is an important word. To understand teaching, it is actual teaching we must study. Watching actual teaching is a wonderful corrective for ungrounded theory-building, much of which consists of "oughts" and "shoulds" disguised as "research" by impenetrable jargon. It is surprisingly rare for theorists to visit actual classrooms. It is a time-consuming and energy-consuming thing to do, and, on top of that, it is often discouraging. It is no wonder that there is such a distance between theorists and classroom teachers. Teachers envy theorists, who can come and go as they please, who have offices of their own, who do not actually do the work day in and day out; and theorists have a hard time imagining the daily reality of an actual classroom. (There are exceptions: *Life in Classrooms* [Jackson 1968] is based on observation, and reformers such as John Holt and Jonathan Kozol write from their own classroom experience. But in the higher reaches of theory-making, observation plays a very small role: A glance over the contents of the Rand McNally *Handbook of Research on Teaching* [Gage 1968] will bear this out.) I have tried, in this study of teaching, to stay in a middle ground between my own experience in the classroom and my work in analytical psychology. Thus there is some autobiography here and in subsequent chapters. I think this mirrors how teaching is actually learned: by doing it, year in and year out. No amount of theory substitutes for doing and then reflecting. Theory can inform and illuminate, but it is no substitute for the daily experience of the classroom. To study teaching we must therefore go and watch teaching being done, and to watch teaching we must visit a school. We begin, then, with such a visit.

Lakeview High School, Chicago. It is 7:30 in the morning of a clear September day. I wedge my way through a crowd of students waiting outside the school's heavy metal double front door. The fact that I'm wearing a tie, and am unknown to them, helps me do my wedging, but I feel their otherness anyway. A grown man surrounded by adolescents is a grown man in alien territory. I pull hard at the heavy door and slip through into a dark entry hall. A teacher doing "door duty" looks up sharply, expecting to have to tell a kid to get back outside until the bell rings, but my tie stills her and she goes back to reading her newspaper. In five minutes she will be engulfed by the mass waiting outside, so she now treasures this moment of peace. I know. I've taught school too. I did it for nine years, and you don't forget these little islands of feeling.

I go down a corridor, past football trophies and color portraits of this year's student council, all in glass display cases better suited to a museum, and into the main office (a sign, MAIN OFFICE, juts out over its door into the hall). Teachers are signing in, using a countertop that divides us from the clerks at their desks and the large, many-windowed office on the other side. Substitute teachers—eight or so—sign special forms and look to see where they will have to be this day. I am here this morning to visit a student teacher, and I tell this to the clerk behind the barrier. I'm handed the "Visitors Sign-In Book," and I sign in, writing "Dan Lindley, UIC [University of Illinois at Chicago], English." "You'll have to wait for Mrs. Marvin to give you your pass," says the clerk. This is new. In past years I've just signed in and been given a card: VISITOR'S PASS. CHICAGO PUBLIC SCHOOLS. DESTI-NATION: ———— . And I don't know who Mrs. Marvin is, either, but I know better than to ask. I assume she's a new assistant principal, doing things by the book. I wait, but I'm anxious. Students will be let in any minute now, and class will begin five minutes after that. The bell indeed rings and the outside corridor becomes a river of students, jostling, calling, banging locker doors—the aliens again.

"I'd like to go on up to the first period class," I say to the clerk. "I'll come back and check in with Mrs. Marvin during division," I say, hoping that by mentioning "division" I'm indicating to the clerk that I know how things work, that I'm an old hand. "Division" is Chicago-ese for "home room" or "attendance period," a time around ten o'clock, carefully selected to guarantee the largest number of warm bodies in attendance, so that the money the state pays the school per body will be as much as possible.

My ploy doesn't work. "You'll have to wait." "Well," I say, "I really don't want to be late for this class. It's my first visit, she knows I'm coming, and she'll be anxious. It wouldn't be fair to her." "You'll have to wait." I think a moment. "Tell Mrs. Marvin that Doctor Lindley will check in with her as soon as he can, but he's gone up on his own to room 311. I'll take the responsibility." And I leave fast. The "doctor" is for pure power, and that's the only reason I ever use it. I'm selfishly glad Mrs. Marvin is *Mrs.* Marvin. If she were a doctor, she'd always be "doctor," in these schools, and I'm already feeling I'll need any dumb advantage I might have when I do see her. (It is a problem involving power: I shall return to it in Chapter 3.)

Room 311 is an odd place: a long, thin space with the teacher's desk in the middle, two floor-to-ceiling windows at one end and the students' seats between her desk and the window. Behind her desk an equal amount of space stretches away with nothing in it except two old filing cabinets, unused, and a few chairs, also unused. I introduce myself to the teacher whose classes my student will be working with and she says things are going well. But the problem with this first period class, she tells me, is that so few students attend regularly. There are twenty-one students assigned, but . . . she shrugs. It's a common situation in these schools. How can you teach students who aren't there? At 7:50, when the bell rings for the beginning of class, six students are chatting and giggling with the slight extra energy that accompanies the start of a new day at school. Now their "regular" teacher sits at her desk, facing the door, and reads some papers or forms she has picked up from her mailbox downstairs in the office. My student, a tall, gangly, friendly young woman, dressed in a peasant blouse and baggy pantaloons that give her a 1960s-hippie look, balances herself on the chair-arm of one of the desks that would otherwise contain a student. "Good morrr-ning," she says, in a singsong way that satirizes school teachers, and the students respond in chorus and in kind. It's a promising beginning. As the class period moves along there will be more students arriving— "tardies," the records will call them. By the time the bell rings to end the class six more students will have shown up, in various states of breathlessness, nonchalance, or sleepiness. That's pretty typical. My student and I will have to work on something you don't hear much about in teacher education programs: how to plan lessons so that a student can arrive any time and become a participant in what's going on.

The students pay no attention to me, a stranger, sitting in the back of the room and occasionally making a note. This is my twenty-fifth year of visiting student teachers, and I still have no idea what to expect from students. Sometimes, as now, I'm ignored. Other times a whole crowd will descend upon me, surrounding me: "You her teacher?" "Is she doin' good?" "We *like* her!" "Give her an A!" and so on. There is a natural alliance between any student teacher and her students. It forms when the students realize that she, too, is a student, and that therefore she too is being evaluated, graded. (Thus my visit reinforces this alliance.) But it will disappear completely with the first day of the first job, because being employed means by definition that one is officially no longer an apprentice, even though one may surely still feel that way. The alliance that comes from being a fellow-student often makes student teaching survivable.

And it's not easy to survive, at the beginning. Teaching is indescribably complex work, so complex that no preparation can be enough. I have never been able to watch a student teacher, especially on my first visit, without remembering my own beginnings as a teacher. I started out, as an undergraduate at Yale in the 1950s, as a zoology major. In my sophomore year, though, I had to take an English course, a survey of ill-assorted works: *Madame Bovary, Paradise Lost, The Love Song of J. Alfred Prufrock*, and many others—neither rhyme (literally) nor reason explained the choices—and by the middle of the year I was hooked. It was Prufrock who got me. I'm an only child, and an introverted only child at that, so I grew up thinking my own thoughts, wrapped up in my own feelings, and here suddenly was Prufrock expressing *my* loneliness. The poem made me aware, for the first time, of my own awareness, and suddenly I saw literature as resonant with my own life. I changed majors, making up for lost time with a summer's work reading modern poetry at Oxford, where I had a particularly clear and demanding teacher and found a miraculously understanding and lovely woman who was my age, and nominally a fellow student, but far more knowledgeable about how books worked. She was years more sophisticated than me, and she became a gentle mentor for me in lovely ways. Between her kindness and the depths of my teacher I was much moved. But a year of graduate work in English at Johns Hopkins was discouraging. I learned something about Old and Middle English and something about how to read Spenser—enough, in fact, that I became a member of the *Faerie Queene* Club, meaning simply that I'd read all of it. But there wasn't much fun, and only occasionally did I feel the sense of discovery—self-discovery, really—that had so involved me at Yale and Oxford. We were a small group of graduate students, all trying to become "scholars." Most of our teachers, though, were hard to see. I made an appointment with one months ahead, at his request, but when I arrived and knocked on his office door he didn't answer. I knew he was in there because smoke from his cigar was drifting out of his office over the transom and into the hall while I waited for him to open the door. He didn't, so I finally trudged back to my stall in the library stacks. This was pretty much the last straw for me, and at the end of the year I quit school and went into the army. I had to do it some time—there was a military draft in those days—so I felt I might as well get it over with. I trained to be a company clerk, at Fort Jackson, South Carolina. All the other trainees on the base jogged everywhere with their rifles and machine guns. We jogged to class with our notebooks at port arms. But when I finished the training and began work as a clerk for a basic training company, people began coming to me for help with writing: How to respond to a postcard from a girlfriend who (the young soldier told me) he knew was cheating on him. How to write to mother. A sergeant who had to write to a finance company because they'd repossessed his refrigerator, along with all his food. Without realizing it,

I was becoming a teacher, and by the time I got out of the army I'd decided to teach school. That was where the real problems were, I'd come to feel. Problems of basic literacy made the world of higher literary studies seem pretty esoteric. So I enrolled in a Harvard MA program designed to make school teachers out of liberal arts graduates.

There were good courses in social policy and philosophy of education, and there was a summer involving a "methods" course and a week of "practice teaching," carefully critiqued by an experienced teacher. But the program I was in made us full-time (and paid) teachers for half a school year instead of giving us a more ordinary "student teaching" experience. Financially it was a good deal, but it meant that we were treated just as if we were experienced teachers: given five classes, hall duty, home room—the whole bit, with almost no supervision. I was assigned to the high school in Natick, a working-class suburb of Boston. I didn't know much about such students, but, I told myself, I'd been to Yale, a fancy graduate school, the army, and now Harvard; I was older, and I thought myself an intelligent and plausible person, so why should I have trouble teaching? But I did. Lots of it.

I couldn't get grounded; I couldn't figure out why things happened. Good classes were followed by raucous ones. Good days were followed by awful ones. A kid would do a wonderful piece of work one day and then defy me the next. Of my five classes, only one made sense every day: It was just a zoo. The department head, Miss Greene, visited and tried to help, but she only made me feel worse. She was a tiny, dumpy lady of a sort you wouldn't notice on the street unless she happened to be a close relative. I would be teaching something, the kids would be noisy or walking around or (the worst thing) just talking quietly among themselves while I was trying to teach, when Miss Greene would walk in. Instantly there would be total silence and rapt attention—to *me*. "Don't talk when Mr. Lindley is teaching," she would say, and leave. The door would shut and the noises would start up again just as before. I couldn't figure it out. What was it about her that made the class suddenly become "good"? What had she done? And how?

One day about three weeks after I'd started I was teaching one of my more difficult classes (but not the zoo) when, with no warning, the whole class applauded. Nothing like this had happened to me before. I was startled and certainly threatened. I thought they'd met before class and conspired to do it: Let's give Lindley the applause treatment, I imagined them saying, and then plotting a time. I put on my severest voice, which wasn't very severe, and demanded to know what was going on. Silence. I demanded again. Silence, and lots of looking down, or at least looking away from me. I demanded again, less urgently. A hand twitched into the air and went right back down, but I'd seen it and I called on its owner. She looked at me shyly. "Mr. Lindley . . ." she began, and then finally she said, "Mr. Lindley, we clapped because you smiled."

I suppose I could have learned something from that. I didn't, though: I stayed tense and anxious. I got through my student teaching, but, I felt, just barely. The school even offered me a position as a regular English teacher for the following year, which made me doubt their judgment even as I was encouraged by the offer. But I knew I couldn't take more of what I'd just been through. Instead I accepted a one-year job at the Groton School, a much older and more prestigious version of the kind of eastern boarding school I'd been a student at myself. I was filling in for a man who had gone on sabbatical—that is why it was a one-year appointment. I liked that arrangement because (I thought) now I can find out if I can really teach, but without any pressure to stay on if I can't. I knew these students (all boys, then) would be polite. They would listen. They wouldn't talk in class. Some of them would be very bright. And all of them would be more or less like me. So I took the job. And taught, happily, for the year.

I then moved on to the laboratory school run by the University of Illinois in Urbana, "Uni High." Here I really began to feel I was getting the hang of it. Then, in my fourth year of teaching, I was visited by a researcher, Bill Rogge, who did something that made me rethink and rework everything I had been doing. He asked if he could visit some of my classes and tape record them. I said sure. Uni was a laboratory school, after all, and such things happened. Later he simply asked me what I thought I was doing: How much did I talk? What kinds of questions was I asking? That sort of thing. It turned out that I—like most teachers—had absolutely no idea. My estimates of what I was doing were wildly off.

I thought, for example, that I talked about 30% of the time in my "gifted" class but about 50% of the time in my "slowest" one. It turned out (and again, this is typical of most teachers) that I talked two-thirds of the time in all my classes. And there was much more I didn't know. So I set about trying to study, with Bill's help, what I was actually doing. It was pretty devastating to reflect that for four years I hadn't had any idea. And most teachers are seldom visited by anyone, let alone someone like Bill. So most teachers are the way I was: They are people of good will, they are trying things, but they have no objective measure of what's actually going on. They have to rely on memory, and memory plays tricks. The biggest trick it plays, of course, is repression.

This first experience at learning to observe myself was the beginning of a long study of the craft. But all during that time I had the sense that something more was involved. The craft could be studied, certainly, but there remained a mystery *under* the craft, and informing it. The mystery slowly emerged from the shadows when, many years later, I began my training in psychoanalysis. In that work, sitting in my office and (for the most part) listening, I was only incidentally a teacher; I was more a companion, albeit one who had traveled just a bit farther. Over time, though, I began to feel that the two of us, patient and therapist, were no longer even separate people, but had fused in some incomprehensible way into a single journeyer. Sometimes I would know the ending of a dream halfway through a patient's telling of it. Sometimes tears would come to my eyes just before a sad or moving account of a bit of a patient's life. In some mysterious way I was becoming equal with my patient: We had descended together into the same archetypal place. Taken over into teaching, I began to see, such a feeling of joining up with a student would lead to a paradox: The goal of teaching is not to teach "well," or dramatically, or even superbly. In fact to try to do so is actually a problem, an over-involvement of ego. Teaching too dramatically, too "effectively," takes up all the space in the classroom. The teacher would outdo the students, so there would be no joining up. And this is a problem. So I began to see that the goal of teaching is to create a situation in which, at a certain (that is, planned-for) moment, the student, who has been working, struggling, and pondering suddenly says, with a mingled sense of elation and loss: "I knew that.

I knew that, all along." Successful teaching, in other words, has to do with what is *already in the student*. This of course is an idea that undermines all the reasons why we have schools and teachers at all, unless we redefine the whole enterprise to conform to the well-known proverb: *When the student is ready, the right teacher appears.*

The problem, of course, is to be the right teacher, with "rightness" being defined by the *student's* inner state. Thus "what" is being taught—the curriculum—needs to resonate with whatever "inner states" we have before us in the classroom. More importantly, the teacher must also resonate, as a person, with these states. This is what my student at Lakeview High School did when she said "good morning" in her singsong way; she acknowledged a certain unreality about the classroom as a place to be, an acknowledgement that must be made if a teacher today is to be credible at all. Schools, as students know perfectly well, are a sort of transitional space between the reality of their lives outside school and the coming reality of life after graduation, or after dropping out. Schools, in other words, are not real in the sense that the "outside" world is real. Instead, schools are places for a sort of serious play, a play of ideas and feelings, joys and fears. Teacher and students share these things, but they also share an acknowledgement, usually tacit, of their unreality. It is this unreality that many experienced teachers have, I believe, come to know intuitively, and they make imaginative, *imaginal* use of it. They have a sense of the child in themselves, so that what they do resonates with the actual child before them, partly because there is a sense of play about what they do when they teach. Further, there is the resonance of synchronicity, of reaching toward, and finding, truth that is both shared and latent, lying as it does in the darkness of the unconscious of each student and each teacher at the level of the archetypal, the collective unconscious as Jung described and defined it. This is true shared ground, because in it both teacher and student are equal.

As I sit in the back of room 311 and make my notes I reflect on these matters. These students will never be in this place in their lives again. Their regular teacher is in a place in her life right now, too. So too is Ms. Shepley, my student. This moment, for this class, for my student and her students, is the "window of opportunity" that is here now and will never come in quite this way again. Most work that adults do is subject to revision, to "fixing." Surgeons can reoperate, lawyers can appeal decisions they feel are wrong, Christmas presents can be returned, the automobile mechanic can try again to find the source of the rattle. But teaching (like psychotherapy) is bound by the circumstances of time and place. The students in this room will grow up; they are growing now—only at this moment are they who they now are. There is only one chance to reach them as they are, and it is right now. Next month, next year, they will be different people. Parents know this for their children, but it is easy for teachers to lose sight of the swiftness of time's passing. An experienced teacher has seen hundreds and hundreds of adolescents over the years, and they begin to seem more alike than different, as indeed they are in many ways. But for any one of them, now is the time, and only now. Only once will they ever read *Huckleberry Finn* for the first time, or try to write something from the life they know at this moment. Thus—to return to the proverb—the student is *always* ready. But for what? And how may we, as teachers, resonate with that readiness?

G. Robert Carlsen, who taught for many years at the University of Iowa and had taught school as well, said to me years ago that teachers go through three stages in their teaching lives. (I have since added a fourth stage, which is the subject of my final chapter.) Carlsen's first stage is simply and solely made up of getting used to being in a room full of children or adolescents. It was the stress of this that had prevented me from smiling, from being naturally human. This is how most teachers remember their first year of full-time (not student) teaching. Any real teaching that happens in this stage—or any learning, for that matter—is purely accidental, serendipitous. The second stage is simply teaching, with some competence, whatever one has been given to teach: the literature anthology, the grammar handbook, the school's curriculum. It is a stage of probation, of being watched and perhaps evaluated by a department chairperson or an assistant principal: a time for toeing the line and keeping one's nose clean. The students give less trouble because they have become more predictable, and because one has developed strategies that handle the little conflicts, accidents, and emergencies. Because of these strategies the feeling of being on pins and needles all the time diminishes. I had arranged to make this stage as easy for myself as possible by moving to a private school. Some teachers stay in this second stage for the whole of their careers. But with any good fortune at all, they will find their way to a third stage.

In the third stage, Carlsen said, the teacher is no longer merely teaching the set curriculum. Gradually the teacher herself is entering the work: She now feels herself to be an original, unique person, with a very particular relationship both to the subject and to her students. Teaching becomes an idiosyncratically creative act, an extension and expression of her whole being. With this come moments of pure joy, or clarity, or fun that were previously only imagined. My experience tells me that this happens, if it ever does, only after three or four years in the classroom. I was helped immeasurably by Bill's visit, but even without it I was on my way to enjoying what I was doing, and enjoying many of my students. Bill's visit helped me reach more of them. Some students from those days still stay in touch, I'm happy to say. Some teachers, though, never achieve this third stage. Some achieve it and then find that it takes so much energy that the rest of their life suffers or is too threatened. They become plain tired, so they retreat insensibly to the second stage in order to stay comfortable, but with a sense of loss and sadness when they remember how they used to do it.

I reflect on all these things as I sit in the Lakeview classroom this September morning. The great problem—largely, I think, unaddressed—in educating teachers is that almost all students who plan to teach do so because they imagine themselves as third-stage teachers *right from the start*. As often as not they have chosen to become teachers not only because they have been inspired by a few excellent teachers of their own but also because they want to do it better than most of the mediocre ones they only vaguely remember. And the ones they only vaguely remember are, of course, those who have stayed in the second stage, going through the motions, but with no involvement, no energy. The students I work with are partly motivated, in other words, by revenge. They, by God, will show the old, tired ones how it's done!

The trouble is it almost never works that way. Almost all of us have had to go through those first two stages. In my experience I've only seen three student teachers, out of hundreds, who were "born" teachers, who were in Carlsen's third stage right from the start. This means that for most of us the earliest experience will have been one of disillusionment or even despair, as mine mostly was. Furthermore my own mentors—Rogge, Carlsen—were for-tuitously encountered, like the magical guides in fairy tales. They weren't part of my formal preparation at all. It is no wonder that half of all the people who train as teachers have left the classroom within five years. The work is that hard to learn, and the learning is that painful.

So as I sit watching my student I reflect on my own journey, and on the journey we teachers all travel in our teaching lives. What are the initiations, the border crossings, the barriers? What is going on, not only in the classroom, but in the teacher? My training as a psychoanalyst has been an inner journey with years' worth of discovery and reflection. We are all, of course, on a journey. It has been my great good fortune to have had, at the right times, guides and mentors—teachers, in the best sense. This book is my bringing together of the two strands of my own working life, teaching and analysis, so as to weave, insofar as it's possible, an outer and an inner reflection on teaching. I'll begin with the "outer," because we need an idea of teaching's public face, of what actually goes on, moment by moment, in classrooms. Of what does the craft of teaching consist?

## WORKS CITED

Gage, Nathan, ed. *Handbook of Research on Teaching*. Chicago: Rand McNally, 1968.
Jackson, Philip. *Life in Classrooms*. New York: Holt, Rinehart and Winston, 1968.

*Chapter Two*

# The Craft of Teaching

*Prospero*:  Lend thy hand,
And pluck my magic garment from me.
So.
Lie there, my art.

—The Tempest, Act 1, Scene 2

The craft, the observable "surface" of teaching, is made up of three domains: (1) asking questions, (2) the flow of talk and whatever else happens by moment, and (3) the curriculum. I'll deal with each of these in turn, but in actual teaching they are fused insensibly together. "Asking questions" is really the patterning of intellectual operations. The flow of events is what determines how the classroom feels. The curriculum is both the manifest curriculum—that is, what is being taught, such as grammar or *Heart of Darkness*—and the "hidden curriculum," Philip Jackson's (Jackson 1968, 36) apt term for the socializing that goes on willy-nilly as students "learn to be passive and to acquiesce to the network of rules, regulations and routines in which [they are] embedded." This chapter will focus on the first domain, questions: specifically, four kinds of questions and the consequences they have for how students and teacher feel about what is happening in the classroom, followed by a discussion of curriculum.

## ASKING QUESTIONS

Ms. Shepley, the student teacher I am visiting at Lakeview, is teaching Ray Bradbury's *Fahrenheit 451* to her little group of six students, the ones who have managed to come to school on time. They have been reading it for a week. Today she begins by asking, "What is Montag's secret?" Let us look closely at this question. In the first place, it contains an assertion, a statement, namely, that Montag *has* a secret. The students know that such a question means that the teacher expects some of them, at least, to know—that is, to remember—what that secret is. School is full of such questions. On the surface they ask for the recall of some fact, something previously discussed. But just watching the class shows that more is going on. Students are scanning one another: Who knows? Who doesn't? Then Maria answers. Maria is the one who always answers, or almost always: She is one of the very few who come every day. "He has books!" she states, and she is pleased with herself. She knows she's right. "That's right. He has books," says Ms. Shepley.

It is a tiny exchange, but it is of such tiny exchanges, hundreds, thousands of them, that teaching consists. And each exchange carries with it a specific charge of feeling, for the teacher, for the student who answers, for the students who knew and would have answered but didn't get a chance, for the students who didn't know and are relieved, even for those who don't care at all. Everything that happens in teaching has at once an intellectual and an emotional dimension: They cannot be separated from one another. Maria feels good. Someone else may feel a bit resentful. Ms. Shepley is probably relieved that Maria answered, partly because I'm watching, but if I had not been there she might have wished that another, less vocal student had taken the chance.

Questions lie at the heart of teaching. Later in this same class Ms. Shepley will tell the students—that is, she will lecture to them—about the phoenix, and how it rises from ashes. Telling has an emotional dimension too, but it is nowhere nearly as vivid as the feelings engendered in the asking of questions. At the moment a question is asked the focus of attention shifts from the teacher to the class, and students know this. Attention always focuses on the teacher when her voice stops. Even students who were paying no attention at all look up: They know something is now expected of them, even if they don't know what. A vague threat hangs in the air, and it is at this moment that students monitor one another. All questions have this bubble of affect around them—some, obviously, more than others. The memory question is especially scary because it is so specific: the answer is either right or wrong. Maria has taken some of her classmates off the hook with her quick response, and they know it and are grateful. Feelings. Questions can't be separated from feelings. Therefore teaching can't be separated from feelings. There is no such thing as "pure" inquiry, "pure" teaching, "pure" ideas. A classroom is never just for "learning." It is a container for a constant flow of feelings: anxiety, glee, boredom, anger, frustration, excitement, pride. And a lot of the flow is shaped by what kinds of questions the teacher is asking.

There are four kinds of questions, and only four. Here I am using the schema in J. P. Guilford's article "The Three Faces of Intellect" (Guilford 1959). The first kind we have already seen: the memory question. It involves only facts, and only the ability to recall. The second kind asks for the kind of thinking Guilford calls *convergent*. If Ms. Shepley had gone on to ask, "*Why* does Montag have books?" she would have asked a convergent question. Convergent questions ask students to take data and reason from them, draw conclusions from them, explain things with them. They are not just about facts, as memory questions are; rather, they are about the *use* of facts. When students ask, "Are we going to have to think today?" it is convergent questions they have in mind.

Ms. Shepley, though, does something else. She divides her little class into two groups of three each and says, "We know how the fire department works in this book, and you know how different it is from what we think fire departments are. So now I'd like you to pick something we know about that isn't in the book, and make up what it would be like." "Can we pick school?" "Sure." "Can we pick a supermarket?" "Sure." And the little groups begin to discuss what to pick, and what things would be like. Soon they add other areas to imagine. The army. Sports competitions where, they decided, the winners would kill the losers in fights to the death.

This is *divergent* thinking. Here the data in the book are no longer anything more than a starting point: The task diverges from the book, hence the term. A question such as this lets students off the cognitive hook and invites them to play around with the subject. "Why does Hamlet reject Ophelia?" is convergent. "What would you have done if you'd been in Hamlet's place?" is divergent.

The fourth and last kind of question is *evaluative*: "Is the society portrayed in this book one you would approve of?" Here a judgment is called for, in this case a political assessment which would ultimately raise the issue of what is a good society. "Was Hamlet right to reject Ophelia?" is evaluative: it asks for a moral judgment. Another sort of evaluative question asks for an aesthetic judgment: "Is this a well-written book?" English teachers, even experienced ones, often make the mistake of asking an evaluative question *first* in a discussion of a piece of literature: "Well, did you like reading this?" Such discussions usually founder because students haven't much skill in backing up their evaluative moves; they've seldom discussed what's good or bad in literature, or why people like or don't like things. So they just blurt out opinions. And judgments, as Hayakawa (1972, 46) writes, stop thought.

Clearly memory questions reward students with an eye for details. They also reward students who find the other sorts of questions threatening in one way or another. Convergent questions reward students with high intelligence—intelligence tests are convergent tasks. Divergent questions reward creative students but seem irrelevant and a waste of time to people whose preference is convergent thinking. Evaluative questions bring out the philosophers, the critics—the judgers.

One of the questions Bill Rogge asked me after he'd gone over the tapes he made of my classes was whether I was interested in stimulating creativity in my classes. I found this question somewhat insulting. Of course I was interested in stimulating creativity in my classes, and I told him so. Then he laid out for me the four kinds of questions, which I'd never heard of before. What kind of questions do *you* ask?, he asked me. I really didn't know, so he told me. I had been asking only memory and convergent questions, in all my classes. There wasn't a single divergent question anywhere. So much for creativity. And there were almost no evaluative questions, either. So much for judgments.

I realized, after I'd gotten over feeling guilty and ignorant, that I asked the types of questions I did—memory and convergent—because that is how I had been taught. The English department at Yale was composed, in my time, of people like Cleanth Brooks and Robert Penn Warren and René Wellek and their disciples, people steeped in what was called New Criticism. New Criticism eschewed the historical and the imaginative and asked, insistently, what the *text* of the work revealed about its own meaning. The meaning had to be figured out from the text alone—in other words, convergently—not from the response of the reader (that would have been divergent or evaluative) and never from imagining what was going on in the mind of the writer (that would have been divergent too). Furthermore, goodness or badness was a matter of the internal, logical consistency in the text. No outside criteria need apply. (That would have been evaluative.) Thus Joyce Kilmer's sappy (pun intended) poem "Trees" ("I think that I shall never see / A poem lovely as a tree") is a bad poem not because it is sentimental (an evaluative notion) but because it is internally inconsistent (a convergent conclusion). One verse, for example, says "A tree whose hungry mouth is prest [sic] / Against the earth's sweet flowing breast," whereas another verse says "A tree that looks to God all day / And lifts her leafy arms to pray." How, my methods teacher at Harvard demanded, could that happen? The mouth down *here* (I made a photo of him bending over) when the arms are up *here*? (The next picture shows him waving his arms in the air, like branches.) It was lots of fun watching him destroy this poem. But it was all convergent, too. So was almost everything he did, thus reinforcing my earlier training. That's where I had learned it, although without knowing what I was learning, and without, of course, any awareness at all of what I was *not* learning.

It is scary to think what teaching with only memory and convergent questions means for a classroom full of students. Some—the thinkers—will of course love it. But the rest, especially the ones who prefer to think divergently or evaluatively, will be left out entirely. They will have to "adapt," as the learning theorists say. But it is an adaptation that for many, probably most, students goes against their true natures. For most students, too, it is an adaptation that drives home the point that teachers are people who don't really know, or care, who their students are. So students learn that they have to play the game of school and go along with that part of the hidden curriculum which is contained in the teacher's unacknowledged preferred ways of doing things. People differ, but a lot of teachers don't honor those differences very well. Some naturally do, of course, but I wasn't one of them.

Jung's theory of psychological types (Jung 1971) illuminates the problem of difference and provides its solution. This is not the place to review this theory in detail, but a basic overview will serve to make the (ultimately) ethical point upon which I want to insist. Jung saw that people define what is most real for them in one of two ways: extraverts (Jung's spelling) find in the outer world their point of reference; it is where they live. Introverts live in the world they create inside themselves. It is true that introverts are often shy and that extraverts are more often outgoing, but this is not the most important consequence of the difference. More important is that we are looking here at two opposed ways of understanding the world and how it works.

Jung began his exploration of psychological types because, characteristically, he knew he needed to understand a most painful experience in his own life, his break with Freud. One by one, Freud's disciples left him and went off on their own. In the context of this study what we are seeing here is the *move away from the teacher*. It is a move predicated on the belief that there is another way to do things, or another way to see and understand. It is illuminating to look at the relationship between Freud the teacher and Jung the student as a paradigm. Freud enabled his followers to work toward an understanding of the then-unknown unconscious. But he did not allow them to see it in ways other than the way he himself did. The same thing happens when a teacher only asks certain kinds of questions and not others.

Between 1896, when the two began corresponding, and 1910, Freud clearly saw Jung as his most talented and important follower. But when Jung deviated from Freud's fundamentally sexual, Oedipal theory of the unconscious in his book *Wandlungen und Symbole der Libido* (Transformations and Symbols of the Libido), the relationship ended, and Jung plunged into a dangerous, lonely exploration of his own unconscious, his own darkness (Jung 1961, 170–99), into what has been called a "creative illness" (Ellenberger 1970, 447–48). But it was no less frightful for being creative, and Jung felt, when he had worked his way through it, that he had to look back at the broken relationship with his former mentor. He had to understand how they differed. He also looked at the break between Freud and another of his pupils, Alfred Adler. As he looked at these other people, Jung came to see himself more clearly.

What he saw was this: Freud had argued that the unconscious is formed when the small child first feels sexual longings for the parent of the opposite sex and murderous wishes toward the (therefore) rival parent of the same sex. These feelings are so terrifying to the child that they are repressed—that is, driven away from the conscious mind—and so they become the unconscious. Thus for Freud the unconscious is formed out of the child's relationships with *other people*—the parents. Because other people are at the core of this theory, Jung saw that Freud's was an extraverted view of what matters in the world: What matters is other people. Adler, by contrast, said that the fundamental drive is not sexual, but rather the *will to power*. The unconscious, for Adler, forms when the will to power produces unacceptable wishes. But the will to power is inside the person, the child doing the willing. This, then, is a theory based on introversion, on the idea that the core of one's being is grown, so to speak, from within. Jung came to see value in both positions, which he called *attitudes*, the two ways of orienting one's psyche. In addition he came to posit four *functions*:

*sensation, thinking, feeling, intuition.* Under sensation I include all perceptions by means of the sense organs; by thinking I mean the function of intellectual cognition and the forming of logical conclusions; feeling is a function of subjective valuation; intuition I take as perception by way of the unconscious, or perception of unconscious contents. (Jung 1971, par. 899)

The parallel with Guilford's four kinds of questions is obvious, although unrecognized by Guilford. The memory question is the domain of the sensation function; evaluative, of feeling; divergent, of intuition; and convergent is thinking. These four functions and two attitudes are, Jung insisted, *preferences*. But they are built-in, innate preferences. And no one function or attitude is "better" than any other; each has its uses, each has its drawbacks. Each, most importantly, is equally valuable. This is the central ethical point. And since we know that our students come to us with varying typologies, we are, I insist, morally obligated to arrange things so that all the students in our class get to do what they prefer, and therefore are best at, at least *some* of the time. This is what I was failing to do. Of course I simply didn't know. And at the end of each year, students—*some* students—would crowd around my desk and say things like, "Oh, I wish I could have you again next year," and they would perhaps even cry a bit, and so would I, and I would go into summer feeling fulfilled and happy. I hadn't noticed that most of the students were just filing out as usual—the end of another class, another year. They hadn't been reached. Not by me, anyway, me with my tasks and rewards for thinkers only.

I mentioned earlier that the biggest problem beginning teachers have is that before they actually begin their student teaching they imagine themselves as fully successful, third-stage teachers. Part of that utopian imagining is the idea that a good lesson will involve, excite, and stimulate everyone in the class. But this almost never happens in real teaching, so this expectation becomes yet another source of disillusionment. Now, I know—and tell my students—that the goal of turning on a light and illuminating the whole class at once is unrealistic. Teaching is more like going into a dark room with a flashlight. You shine the beam around and eventually you know what's in the room. Questions are like that. If one has planned so as to use *all four* kinds of questions, one can at least take solace in the conviction that one has tried to shine some light on each student at least some of the time. The beam of a convergent question hits some students but not others, but some of those others will light up with evaluative questions, and so on. And they are not better or worse students; they just differ from one another, as Jung insisted. So a reasonable and realistic goal for a teacher is to try to "light up" each student in the class *some* of the time during a day, a week, a school year.

For four years I taught as if my way, convergent thinking, was the only way "English" was to be learned, or understood. It wasn't that I was arbitrary or stubborn, but simply that I knew no other way. If there is a moral imperative to walk a mile in the other's moccasins, I was ignoring it. This issue has a deeper level, too, in Jung's typology. Jung saw that people had one preferred (or "dominant") function, and that this preference meant that the opposite function was unfamiliar-seeming and awkward. The opposite of thinking is feeling; of sensation, intuition. So if I ask a feeling-type person a convergent question he will not only do poorly, but he will feel uncomfortable, inadequate to the task, frustrated, maybe even angry. Most students don't express such emotions, though, they just get sulky and quiet. Another part of the "deeper" aspect of typology is what extraverts and introverts do with the function they prefer. Introverts, as you might expect, use their preferred function to get in touch with their own inner selves. They don't use it much in the outside world at all. Instead, they use one or other of the "auxiliary" functions. For example, an introverted person whose dominant function is sensation will use that function inside herself, monitoring with exquisite attention her inner mental and physical states. And she will use either thinking or feeling to do her school work, which is of course done in the "outside" world. The soul of an introvert is a very private place indeed, seldom made visible to teachers, although there may be glimpses in journal work or in an occasional "shock of recognition" triggered by a piece of literature. When I read *Prufrock* for the first time I was shocked to find out that what I had been doing all my life—exploring my own inner world—was done by others too. More precisely, I discovered introverted feeling. Prufrock was haunted, as I was, by the introverted feeling person's root question: Does my life *matter*?

Extraverts, on the other hand, use their dominant function to connect with the outer world around them. Their dominant function is up front and visible. Ronald Reagan was an extraverted feeling type: He had no trouble making clear how he stood on an issue. But thinking (figuring things out) and sensation (mastering the details) presented real problems for him. With extraverts you know what's what. With introverts, you don't get things so clearly put forth. They tell the truth, but they tell it slant—through an auxiliary function. Jimmy Carter, an introverted thinking type, understood things much better than Reagan did but was much less successful at selling his ideas to Congress—or to the people. And one more thing. Most English teachers, like most psycho-therapists, are introverted. Literature led them to discover things inside themselves, and those discoveries were so compelling that they became teachers so as to pass along the experience of their inner journey. (Introverts can be successful as teachers even though teaching looks like a public, showy, extraverted thing to do, because the classroom is such a safe place for an introvert to act "out of character." It feels a lot safer in there than it does in the real world.) But the fact that most English teachers are introverted makes for a problem in the classroom, because most of the popu-lation of the United States, around 80% (Meyers 1980, 157ff.), is extraverted. No wonder English teachers are regarded as slightly off by parents and students alike. What's more, if the teacher is an introverted feeling type (driven by an inner sense of values), she will be in direct conflict with the prevailing typology of the ado-lescent subculture—particularly the inner city variety—which is extraverted sensation. Sensation function people live for the mo-ment, whereas feeling types live in a world of eternally estab-lished values and norms. Feeling-type teachers say things like, "You may not understand this now, but some day . . . ," while the extraverted sensation student is wanting the thing to matter right now or not at all. To teach such students successfully a teacher *must* imagine what the extraverted sensation person's world is like, even if she does not or cannot choose to live in it. One way to get a sense of it is to watch students during lunch, or at a basket-ball game. In such settings their exquisite sense of detail, of what is happening in front of them, becomes manifest and can be ad-mired. As I stood outside Lakeview High School, part of my feeling of being an alien being came from this difference. The students are all crowded around paying attention to what's going to happen immediately as the doors open for them: who they will see before class, whether they will have time to get to a boy-friend's locker to give him a candy bar. I, on the other hand, was thinking about teaching in the abstract, and about why it mattered for me to see my student. Different worlds. Not better or worse worlds, just different. But the difference must be bridged. Rafael

Lopez-Pedraza (a Jungian analyst) once remarked that Jung should have won the Nobel Peace Prize for *Psychological Types*. It is a book that celebrates difference by making no judgments about what is better or worse. It says instead that people differ naturally, and that this is a fundamental fact of human nature. Teachers and educators talk about "individual differences" a lot, but in actual practice they reward only the students who resemble themselves.

## THE FLOW OF FEELINGS

We have seen that even a simple memory question triggers off a wide array of feelings in a class. Those students who know the answer feel one way, those who don't, another; those who put their hands up differ in attitude from those who know the answer but don't volunteer, and so on. How a teacher *responds* to what happens in class is just as important as what a teacher *does*. Students and teachers are brought together in schools precisely because they are in an important sense not equals. The teacher is assumed to have some dominion over her charges because, at the very least, she is older than they are. And because she knows curriculum. And because she is "trained" to teach. These are the things taxpayers pay for. But since students have never been noted for their subservience to their elders—since, in fact, adolescence is all about freeing one's self from one's elders—there will always be tension in classrooms. How the teacher deals with this tension is crucial to her success.

We must go and observe actual teaching to see how this problem is managed. No amount of theory or advice will substitute for studying what actually happens in classrooms. Most teachers almost never have the chance to watch teaching being done. School schedules don't allow for cross-visitation, for one thing, and for another, actual teaching is so demanding that a free period is a time for recharging one's battery, not for watching someone else's struggles. Furthermore, most teachers are uncomfortable with observers. One reason for this is that most observers aren't really trained, as Bill Rogge was, to actually *observe* and then report what they factually saw. Most observers do not really observe. Rather, they sit and imagine what they would be doing up there and compare that with what they are seeing. This is not observing, in my sense of the word, at all. It is simply an invitation to a contest of wills. What is lacking in most observing is a method of recording what is actually happening. The four kinds of questions yield one such method. One could simply record what kinds of questions are in use and then ask the teacher, as Bill asked me, whether what I was doing (convergent questions only) matched what I wanted to be doing, which was more divergent and evaluative.

In general, a good observing strategy is to ask the teacher, before class, for some specific act or behavior that she thinks she is using, or would like to use. Asking divergent questions, for example. Then the observer keeps track of the kinds of questions that are actually being asked. When the class is over the observer asks the teacher what she thought happened—her *estimate* of what occurred. She might say, for instance, that more than half of her questions were divergent ones. Then the observer can tell her what actually happened—that she asked twelve divergent questions, eight convergent questions, and eight memory questions, for example. This observation sets up three very important and separate variables wanting attention: the teacher's *ideal* (what she wanted to do); the teacher's *estimate* of what she actually did; and, finally, what she in fact *actually* did. Ideal, estimate, actual. The definition of a truly accomplished teacher would be a person who can bring these three into agreement, moment by moment, in the classroom. Most teachers are not in a position to work on this central task because there is no one to observe them objectively and thereby to help them in this way. A third-stage teacher is a teacher who can make a plan and then know whether that plan was accomplished or not. It sounds simple. But the utter isolation in which teaching is done makes this simple task almost impossible. Most teachers believe that what they think is happening *is* what is happening. The research overwhelmingly contradicts this belief. The fact is that *most teachers don't know* (as I didn't know) *and most observers don't know how to help them to know.* Instead they just overlay their own (erroneous) idea of what they think they ideally do upon the observed teacher's (erroneous) idea of what she has just done. It is a true pedagogic *folie à deux.*

What is needed is an objective way of describing what happens in teaching. One such method was developed by Ned A. Flanders (1970). Flanders calls his technique "Interaction Analysis." He hypothesizes that the teacher's talk is what accounts for the feeling tone in a class, or, to use his term, the "classroom climate." An observer using this technique writes down, every three seconds (and every time a change from one category to another occurs) a number, which represents (arbitrarily) a particular kind of utterance. Thus the number one indicates that the teacher has verbally accepted a student's feeling. A number eight indicates that a student has spoken in response to something the teacher has done, such as asking a question. Interaction Analysis records only verbal occurrences. There are seven categories (numbered one through seven) of teacher talk, two categories (numbered eight and nine) of student talk, and a tenth category for "silence or confusion." The chart in the appendix to this chapter describes these categories in more detail. For Flanders the distinction between indirect teacher influence and direct teacher influence is especially important. Indirect influence involves accepting feelings, encouraging students, and asking questions. Direct influence is lecturing, giving directions, and making corrections either to student responses or student behaviors.

The series of numbers representing an observation is coded into a ten by ten matrix. By way of illustrating the technique involved, it is useful to imagine a much-simplified system. For example, suppose that all teacher talk could be divided into two broad categories: accepting of students, and rejecting of students. (These categories are too global and too subjective, of course, to be of actual use. My point here is simply to illustrate how the matrix is constructed and how it comes to reveal what it does.) If we use *A* as the symbol for acceptance and *R* for rejection, and if we write down either the one or the other every three seconds as we listen to the teacher teaching, then we might (for example) obtain this thirty-second pattern:

*A*

*A*

*A*

*A*

*R*

*R*

A

A

R

A

The matrix is constructed by entering pairs of these symbols in a table. The table for this two-category system would appear as follows:

|     | A | R |
| --- | --- | --- |
| A |   |   |
| R |   |   |

The technique for creating a matrix involves treating each item first as an entry in a row and next as an entry in a column of the matrix. Thus the first pair of As in our sequence above is represented by one mark in the "Row A–Column A" box. The second A is then used to designate a row and the third a column, then the third a row and the fourth a column, the fourth a row and the fifth a column, and so on. Tallying our sequence in this way, we have:

|     | A | R |
| --- | --- | --- |
| A | 4 | 2 |
| R | 2 | 1 |
| Totals: | 6 | 3 |

It is now possible to look at the numbers in each cell while at the same time considering what each cell means. The top left cell (A,A) reflects entries made only when one "accepting" remark was followed by another accepting remark, or when one such remark continued for more than three seconds. The bottom right cell represents the same thing for "rejecting" remarks. The other two cells represent transitions in either direction: from A to R (top right) or from R to A (bottom left). In addition to learning something from each cell, the totals enable us to calculate a ratio of accepting to non-accepting remarks: in this case, two to one. One has only to imagine the actual ten-by-ten matrix to understand what a wealth of information it contains. We no longer have a narrative account of events. Rather, each cell tells us what did or did not happen and the frequency with which each event occurred. Thus, for example, we could know, for a given class, that if a student initiated something ("nine") it was likely to be accepted (the "nine-three" cell), but it wasn't encouraged (if we see no tallies in the "nine-two" cell). Again, if there are many tallies in the "nine-seven" cell, that teacher tends to punish student initiatives. So the matrix is a kind of "emotional map" of a class. It is a very powerful and discriminating instrument indeed.

I have seen experienced teachers who, for example, never verbally accepted any student's response or encouraged any student to continue talking. Rather, if an answer was acceptable they moved right on to the next question, and if an answer was wrong they would always ask the same question of another student. In their matrices there were no ones, twos, or threes. There was, needless to say, a rather high level of anxiety in their classes. And it was an anxiety of which they were largely unaware.

Flanders' research has shown that most teachers teach in the same way (that is, produce very similar matrices) day in and day out, in all their classes, and that this patterning is independent of curriculum or student ability level or even class size. Of course most teachers would vehemently deny this, but I am persuaded of it both by the research and by my own experience. Because he had used the Flanders technique, Bill Rogge knew how much I talked and how much my students talked. He asked me, before he told me, whether I talked more in my brightest class than in my slowest one. "No," I told him. "I don't have to talk much with the bright class. They do all the talking. But in my slow class," I said, "it's more like pulling teeth." "How *much* do you talk in those classes?" he asked me. I told him I thought I talked about a third of the time in my brightest class and about half the time in my slowest one.

As I noted before it turned out I was talking about two-thirds of the time in *both* classes. I simply had no idea. I was completely unaware of what I was actually doing. Other studies have had similarly devastating results. One researcher (William Snyder, personal communication) found that science teachers interacted the same way with two students working at a laboratory station as they did with thirty students in regular instruction. I found, while collecting data for my dissertation (Lindley, 1970), that English teachers teach grammar with the same patterns they use to teach poetry and creative writing. The fact is that most teachers settle into a preferred way of doing things and, once they do, it *never changes*. In effect—and this is a huge part of the hidden curriculum—students are sent the message that how their teacher teaches has nothing to do either with them or the curriculum. I believe that part of learning to teach, then, *must* involve developing the ability to make conscious changes in how one goes about interacting with students. It is no wonder students don't care much about what is being taught them, but instead care a great deal about who is doing the teaching. They have learned, the hard way, that the classroom is seldom a place where they can shape in any way the responses they need. Rather it is a place where things are as they are because of the teacher. In this way it resembles an unresponsive home.

One thing I slowly began to learn to do, after Bill's work with me, was to ask divergent questions. At first it was very hard. I thought I was wasting my time and my students' time. Who cared what they would do if they were in Ophelia's place? Wasn't Ophelia what mattered? But as I became slowly more comfortable with such questions I noticed that students who hadn't ever spoken up in class before were beginning to do so. That made me feel a little better. And as I felt better I changed a bit more. I saw that if I asked some divergent questions then more students would talk, and if more students talked I felt better, and so on. The mystery that had haunted me since Natick, of why things happened in class as they did, was beginning to get cleared up. Things happened because of what I was doing, and I had to know what that was in order to get a handle on things. Change, I found, breeds more change. Hobart Mowrer, a University of Illinois psychologist, once said that "We do not think our way into new ways of acting; we act our way into new ways of thinking." So the way to learn about teaching is to do new things and know that one is doing them. I had begun to see that I could plan a lesson and then teach so that the students would in fact talk two-thirds of the time.

They'd do it because I'd wait for them to do so. I was learning to set an ideal for myself and then to have a pretty good idea, after the class, whether I'd carried it out or not. I taped my classes for a year to help myself do this. It is this procedure, I think, that should be at the core of learning the craft of teaching. It involves practicing the task of setting up an ideal, doing the teaching, estimating what one has done, and then comparing the ideal, the estimate, and the actual. It isn't that one gets all three to match all the time; that would be utopian. It's the humbler objective of knowing what one is in fact doing. Only then can changes be made. Only then can one be direct for some of the time and indirect at other times, and ask all the kinds of questions, and so on. Only then is one in command of the craft. Only then is a teacher meeting the needs of all the students some of the time, rather than some (only a few, probably) of the students all of the time. Mastering the craft is, then, an exercise in becoming aware of what one is actually doing, moment by moment. It is *not* a question of "mastering" the curriculum, the knowledge of the subject being taught, paradoxical as this may seem. I turn now to this issue.

## THE CURRICULUM

The lay public, and a great many school administrators and teachers as well, think of the curriculum—by which I mean simply what is being taught—as the real center of teaching. In this model the teacher is a purveyor of "material," or the student is an empty vessel who needs to be filled with what adults deem useful or important. At no time in the recent history of American education was this view taken more seriously than during the so-called "Sputnik Crisis" and the subsequent report of the Woods Hole Conference sponsored by the National Academy of Sciences. This report (Bruner 1960) emphasized the idea that not only was there "structure" inherent in the various academic disciplines but that it could be "discovered" by students given appropriate curricula. Thus, given a true insight into the structure of a subject, it should be possible, Bruner suggested, to design ways of teaching that subject so that students would gain the same insight for themselves. Teaching thus creates—or is supposed to create—the feeling, in students, that they are replicating those processes of

thought by which insights into the various disciplines were first
gained by specialists. Bruner wrote,

Intellectual activity everywhere is the same, whether at the frontier of
knowledge or in a third grade classroom. What a scientist does at his desk
or in a laboratory, what a literary critic does in reading a poem are of the
same order as what anybody else does when he is engaged in like activities—if he is to achieve understanding. The difference is in degree, not in
kind. The schoolboy learning physics *is* a physicist, and it is easier for him
to learn physics behaving like a physicist than by doing something else.
(14)

This was, at the time, heady stuff. And, starting with PSSC
Physics, very large and expensive curriculum-design projects got
underway all across the United States. To be sure, the emphasis
was at first on the sciences, mathematics, and foreign languages,
because that was where we were seen to be lagging behind the
Russians. But the moneys available from Washington were so
lavish that some trickled down as far as English, and a number of
"Project English" curriculum centers were established. The influence of Bruner's report was manifest. Here, for example, is a
passage from the preface to the Oregon Project English curriculum
materials:

The "New English"—and the Oregon curriculum—differs in two other
respects also from the traditional English program. First, behind all the
several varieties of "New English" lies the desire to present to school
children of whatever age only knowledge that is accurate and honest,
knowledge that, even when presented in the most elementary form, is true
to the facts as they are known at the most advanced levels of research. . . .
    The second important difference between the "New English" and the
conventional English program is the effort made by the former to discover
a workable sequence for English instruction and to make the curriculum
from year to year both sequential and cumulative. . . . The Oregon Curriculum, in pursuing this objective, has attempted—we think with some
success—to adapt Jerome Bruner's notion of the "spiral" to the English
curriculum. We have selected a few of the organizing principles of literature or rhetoric or grammar, as the case may be, those principles which
give structure and identity to the particular branch of knowledge, and
have presented these principles through simple applications in the early

years and more complex and sophisticated applications as the child grows older. (Kitzhaber, v-vi)

Here clearly is a description of an effort to find a structure and a sequence, to decide what is to be taught, and when. But a close reading of these passages shows, too, that it is the curriculum itself, and not the teacher, which is taken to be the active agent in the instruction. Thus there are phrases such as "the desire to *present* to school children of whatever age only knowledge that is accurate and honest" (italics added). But, as we have seen, "presenting" is the least of a teacher's actual activities; the implication here, anyway, is that the curriculum does the presenting, which of course cannot be the case. Again, the "New English" is said to "discover," to "reinforce," to "acquaint," and, elsewhere, to "influence literary taste." The curriculum (not the teacher) is seen as active. In fact one of the fantasies of the whole curriculum reform movement of the early sixties was to create "teacher-proof" curricula which would, in some fashion, teach themselves. Underlying this effort, it now seems clear, was a need on the part of many university faculty members, the "experts," to dictate curriculum content to the (inferior) folks who hadn't made it into higher academic settings, but who were laboring in the vineyards of their high school and (even more strange) junior high school classrooms. This is an issue of the power shadow discussed in Chapter 5.

The early sixties were the high water mark of curriculum work in this country: more people, more places, more money. In English, all but one of the federally funded curriculum centers did what Oregon did: They developed their own best idea of *the* English curriculum. One, however, was very different. At Florida State University, a group under Dwight Burton set out to develop and then test the relative effectiveness of three *separate* curricula. The three were based on the following three principles of organization, as described in the U.S. Office of Education Final Report (U.S.O.E. 1968):

1. A series of instructional units centered on definite facets of subject matter in literature, composition, and the English language [the "tri-component" curriculum].

2.  A series of themes reflecting the four basic humanistic relationships: man and deity; man and other men; man and nature; man and his inner self [the "thematic" curriculum].
3.  A sequential step and process approach to the facets of language, literature and composition [the "cognitive process" curriculum]. (3)

After these three curricula had been designed (together with explicit directions to the teachers who were to teach them), the following procedures were carried out:

1.  Subject selected groups of students from six Florida junior high schools to three experimental curricula for a three year period.
2.  Test the effects of the curricula by administering a comprehensive evaluation program to the students in the experimental group and to those in a comparable control group.
3.  Draw inferences and form recommendations on the basis of analysis of the data gathered in the evaluation program. (20)

The people engaged in writing the three experimental curricula—experienced teachers together with graduate students, all of whom also had school teaching experience—became genuinely engaged in their task. Each group developed the conviction that its approach made the most sense, had the most cogent structure, and would therefore prove superior to the others. Friendly rivalries developed. Each group came to resemble a sort of miniature Project English team, engaged in designing "the" curriculum for grades seven, eight, and nine. I became involved with this study near its end, and I remember becoming convinced that the "thematic" curriculum would win out for sure. We were all partisans of one or another of them—probably, I now realize, because of our various typologies. Feeling types would like the thematic, because the themes "mattered." Thinking types preferred the Cognitive Process curriculum, naturally.

At the end of each year, students in the three experimental curricula and in the control group (students who were taught the regular English curricula already in place in the project schools) were tested for skills and content knowledge. Their feelings about each curriculum were also assessed by means of a semantic differential instrument. While some differences between the experimental groups and the control group did emerge, nevertheless, in general,

The analysis of variance of the data obtained from the objective test battery, the sentence-combining test [a test of the ability to use grammatical concepts], and the controlled writing problems indicates that *none of the four groups dominated another* (i.e., at the .01 level). (126, italics added)

But the really significant conclusion from the Florida State study, from the standpoint of what actually happens in classrooms, is the following:

The schools factor represented to a large extent the inevitable teacher variable, and the results of the various tests . . . show this factor to be consistently *very* significant. One might have expected this phenomenon to have occurred, but it invites speculation. . . . The schools factor in the analysis of variance would seem to indicate that differences between teachers played a critical role in the success or failure of the several programs tested in the study.

Much of the effort in the field of English in the last decade has been directed toward development of subject matter and the sequence in which it is to be presented. Curricula often have been devised independently of the teachers who are to teach [them]. There seems to be an assumption that if a curriculum is carefully prepared and teachers are given explicit directions on how to proceed, the outcomes for students will be largely similar regardless of the teacher. The results of the Florida State study suggest that a teacher-proof curriculum is an elusive quantity, perhaps unattainable. The period of curriculum development . . . might well have run its course. *It may be time to answer a new and more compelling question: What is an English teacher? How, in other words, does an English teacher's behavior contribute to the success of the students in his class?* (128, italics added)

Nothing in the years since this study was completed has done anything to change my conviction that this conclusion is entirely justified. The curricula—all of them, experimental ones or the control group one—simply made no difference. This is not to say that curriculum is of no importance: Schools obviously have to teach something, and that something should be organized usefully and should consist of interesting, quality materials. The fallacy is in the assumption that there will be a connection between what is taught and what actually happens in the teaching. The flow of feelings, the kinds of questions, the management of those moments when students and teacher are connected or estranged—indeed, almost all the things that make teaching work or not work—originate *within the teacher herself.*

Let us return once more to the beginning of Ms. Shepley's class. The fact that Ms. Shepley sat casually out among her students, on one of "their" desks, mattered. And she seemed comfortable doing this. Another person might have felt very anxious out there, and so would not have done such a thing, but rather would have remained standing, or stayed behind the teacher's desk. One teacher makes a connection with young people by being informal, like the young people themselves. Another makes the connection through authority, through knowledge. Either will work. But where do these differences come from? For an answer we must turn our attention to the inner world of the teacher, for it is here that not only the teacher-student relationship, but all teaching, is in some way shaped. We must leave, then, the comfortable world of classroom observation and lesson planning, the whole sphere of visible technique and craft. We enter now the domain of psyche.

## WORKS CITED

Bruner, Jerome S. *The Process of Education.* Cambridge, Massachusetts: Harvard University Press, 1960.

Ellenberger, Henri F. *The Discovery of the Unconscious.* New York: Basic Books, 1970.

Flanders, Ned A. *Analyzing Teacher Behavior.* Palo Alto, California: Addison-Wesley, 1970.

Guilford, J. P. "The Three Faces of Intellect." *American Psychologist* 14 (1959): 469–79.

Hayakawa, S. I. *Language in Thought and Action.* New York: Harcourt Brace Jovanovich, 1972.

Jackson, Philip. *Life in Classrooms.* New York: Holt, Rinehart and Winston, 1968.

Jung, C. G.. *Memories, Dreams, Reflections.* New York: Pantheon Books, 1961.

————. *Psychological Types.* Vol. 6 of *The Collected Works of C. G. Jung.* 20 vols. Princeton, New Jersey: Bollingen Series XX, Princeton University Press, 1971.

Kitzhaber, Albert R. *The Oregon Curriculum, A Sequential Program in English: Literature I.* New York: Holt, Rinehart and Winston, 1967.

Lindley, Daniel A., Jr. "Rhetorical Analysis of Teaching in Selected English Classrooms." Ph.D. Diss. Florida State University, 1970.

Meyers, Isabel Briggs. *Gifts Differing*. Palo Alto, California: Consulting Psychologists Press, 1980.

U.S. Office of Education, Bureau of Research. *Final Report Project No. H-026: The Development and Testing of Approaches to the Teaching of English in the Junior High School*. Tallahassee: Florida State University, 1968.

## APPENDIX: FLANDERS INTERACTION ANALYSIS CATEGORIES

### Teacher Talk: Indirect

1. *Accepts feeling.* Accepts and clarifies an attitude or the feeling tone of a pupil in a nonthreatening manner. Feelings may be positive or negative. Predicting and recalling feelings are included.

2. *Praises or encourages.* Praises or encourages pupil action or behavior. Jokes that relieve tension, but not at the expense of another individual, saying "Um hm," or "go on" are included.

3. *Accepts or uses ideas of pupils.* Clarifying, building, or developing ideas suggested by a pupil. Teacher extensions of pupil ideas are included, but as the teacher brings more of his ideas into play, shift to category five.

4. *Asks questions.* Asking a question about content or procedure, based on teacher ideas, with the intent that a pupil will answer.

### Teacher Talk: Direct

5. *Lecturing.* Giving facts or opinions about content or procedures, expressing *his or her own* ideas, giving *his or her own* explanation, or citing an authority other than a pupil.

6. *Giving directions.* Directions, commands, or orders with which a pupil is expected to comply.

7. *Criticizing or justifying authority.* Statements intended to change pupil behavior from nonacceptable to acceptable pattern; bawling someone out; stating why the teacher is doing what he or she is doing; extreme self-reference ("In thirty years of teaching, I've never seen anything so silly").

### Pupil Talk

8. *Pupil talk—response.* Talk by pupils in response to teacher. Teacher initiates the contact or solicits pupil statements or structures the situation. Freedom to express own ideas is often limited.

9. *Pupil talk—initiation.* Talk by pupils which they initiate. Expressing own ideas; initiating a new topic; freedom to develop own ideas and a line of thought, like asking thoughtful questions; going beyond the existing structure.

## Silence or Confusion

10. *Silence or confusion.* Pauses, short periods of silence, and periods of confusion in which communication cannot be understood by observer. (Flanders 1970, 34)

*Chapter Three*

# The Source of Good Teaching

*Prospero*:  (Aside to Ariel) My Ariel, chick,
That is thy charge: then to the elements
Be free, and fare thou well!
—*The Tempest*, Act 5, Scene 1

What is good teaching? There is, of course, no single answer. There are at least a thousand—who knows how many more—ways of teaching well. We do know, however, when we are in the presence of good teaching. We feel its energy in the classroom: We see students alert, involved; we see a teacher who is demanding, compassionate, funny, original. We know, watching, that something special is happening. The students know it too. So do other teachers in the school; they know who the "good teachers" are. Whatever it is that those good teachers do becomes visible in special relationships between teacher and students. Good teaching has to do with how these relationships begin and how they grow. What is the source of this good work, this special energy that seems to buoy the class along? This chapter first sets forth a theoretical approach to the source of good teaching. This is followed by a return to Lakeview High School, together with further examples, to illustrate the theory.

## THE KNOWING ADULT/UNKNOWING CHILD ARCHETYPE

Consider the word "source." Its etymological origin is "to spring forth, to rise," and that suggests a spring, water rising from the earth, the source of a river. Water nourishes: In the end it makes life possible. Thus our subjects are origin, and movement, and nourishing, and their connections with teaching and with our lives as teachers. Teaching, like water, nourishes. May we trace teaching to its source?

The shared characteristics of good teaching suggest that it has a common energy source. All good teaching has an element in it that binds teacher and students together. Somehow they have linked up, they have made common cause. They find joy in what is happening. Both are "motivated," "excited," "concerned," "involved." Good teaching is not done *to* students; it is done *with* them. Whereas ordinary teachers sometimes, or often, feel anxious in class because they sense a separation between themselves and their students, good teachers feel like students themselves: They are excited by the newness of old ideas.

The quest for the source of this excitement might very well begin with the question, What drew us into teaching in the first place? It is worth stopping for a time to ponder our answer. What were our feelings about our early teachers? Did we enjoy being with or taking care of younger children? Or perhaps we weren't drawn: Perhaps we were pushed. Our parents wanted us to be teachers and told us so. We were told how "wonderful" it would be if we were to become a teacher. The same thing happens, of course, in the families of some doctors, priests, lawyers, and gymnastics champions. Being pushed can create problems, but they're not necessarily fatal: I've known many students who've done well in spite of such pressure. When things do go wrong, though, such parental pressure is often part of the reason. The student herself does not own the decision to go into teaching, for one thing. And for another thing, the parents may be more interested in their-son-or-daughter-the-teacher than they are in their son or daughter as a person. Their real reason for pushing their child is to give their own self-esteem a boost. Some of the saddest people in the world are those whose lives have been lived in the service of their parents' narcissistic needs. When such people become teachers they are invariably disillusioned because they were never "illusioned" about teaching in the first place: They never wanted to do it, either for themselves or for their students.

Fortunately, they are the exception, not the rule. Far more often the choice of teaching is genuine. For many teachers of English, the attraction to teaching came from the experience of a piece of literature together with an excellent teacher in magical connection. Such was my experience with *Prufrock*. My teacher had the sense to stay out of my way and let me write a sophomoric paper (I was a sophomore) about it. Later he taught me some discipline. Another reason some people go into teaching is the attraction of the prospect of doing important work essentially alone—that is to say, not in the presence of other adults. Teaching is a way of staying out of the hurly-burly of competitive worldly work. David C. McClelland (1953) found that of all the occupational groups (and he studied many of them) school teachers had the lowest "need for achievement," meaning, roughly, ambition. (Risk-taking entrepreneurs had the highest, as one might expect. Bankers were in the middle range, and so on.) I will soon return to this idea, that teachers are not quite members of normal adult society.

In any event teachers can, for the most part, set their own standards for themselves. There are no external rewards for good teaching (merit pay is a dying idea) and no punishments for bad teaching. Everyone just goes up the union-negotiated pay scale year by year, regardless. So there are a lot of possible reasons why people become teachers. But none of these, I believe, get to the heart of the issue. There is a deeper, less conscious, essentially archetypal reason for teachers entering the profession. It may not apply to all. I am sure, though, that it applies to most of the ones who teach well.

Being a teacher means that one is always in the presence of young(er) people. Indeed, they stay the same age year after year. Very few occupations have this sameness-of-client aspect to them: Pediatrics qualifies, and so for the most part does undertaking, but that's about it. Most people enter a life work and grow older along with the clientele they serve. But for teachers it's another crop of tenth graders each year, different by face and name but similar to last year's in temperament, in adolescent turmoil, in attention span, and in beliefs. This sameness would drive most people crazy. How do teachers stand it, let alone welcome it? This is a question we ask ourselves, and it is sometimes asked—and more often thought—of us by the lay public as well. It is an exceptionally important question because whether we enjoy teaching and therefore keep on doing it depends upon our answer. Here, then, is that deeper archetypal answer:

The archetype by which the good teacher is fascinated is that of the knowing adult–unknowing child. A good teacher must stimulate the knowing adult in each child, so to speak. . . . But this can only happen if the teacher does not lose touch with his own childishness. In practical terms this means, for example, that he must not lose spontaneity in his teaching and must let himself be guided somewhat by his own interests. He must not only transmit knowledge but must awaken a thirst for knowledge in the children, and this he can do [only] if the knowledge-hungry, spontaneous child is still alive within him. (Guggenbuhl-Craig 1979, 105–6)

In the following chapters I will explore more thoroughly the Jungian concept of archetypes. For now, a passage from Jung will suffice: "In every adult there lurks a child—an eternal child, something that is always becoming, is never completed, and calls for unceasing care, attention and education. That is the part of the human personality that wants to develop and become whole" (Jung 1954, 169–70).

The source, then—the source of the energy that drives good teaching—is the child in the teacher. This idea explains the bond that forms between the good teacher and her students. The students feel they have a kindred child, a colleague, in their teacher. But, *because that inner child is as playful and as irresponsible as they are, they—the students—must gear up an adult part of themselves to take care of (indeed, to teach) the child-in-the-teacher.* Thus students act more responsibly, stay more alert, and become, in part, not learners but teachers. For what the Guggenbuhl-Craig passage posits is that teachers and students are both split into two parts. Each teacher has a conscious, out-in-the-world teacher self as well as an unconscious inner child. And each student has an unconscious inner adult. This idea is the basis of all that I am about to say.

Sometimes the teacher's inner child is absent or has died. But in this chapter I want to assume that the inner child is alive and well and that, like any child, it thrives on attention. If good teaching is driven by that child, by what happens when the eager learner in the teacher calls forth the knowing adult in the student, then poor teaching has the opposite feeling to it. Poor teaching—the shadow of good teaching—is teaching through the use of power alone. Power is easy for teachers to use: threatening a test or a pop quiz, giving grades with no clear rationale, or, more subtly, determining who is noticed or not noticed in a class. Indeed the whole school is a hierarchy of power, as that Lakeview High School secretary was at some pains to remind me. But power in one place makes people in another place vulnerable. A learner is especially vulnerable: The learner is by definition ignorant of something and may therefore be found out. Specifically, learners are "found out" when they act like children—when they are loud or impulsive, for example. When students are not made to feel like adults who can join up with and help the teacher, true learning ceases, and teacher and students go around and around, each trapped in their ordinary and conventional public roles, with power and powerlessness appropriately assigned, alas, to each: power to the teacher, powerlessness to the student.

There are two kinds of teaching: teaching driven by the will, and teaching driven by imagination. Although they often overlap in real classrooms, they may be separated for the purpose of analysis and reflection. Teaching driven by the will is teaching that uses power. Such teaching is often claimed to be imitative of the "real world," which is assumed to be a place where power rules. Teaching driven by the imagination, on the other hand, sees the mastery of the subject as a step toward independence. The teacher imagines competence in her students; that is, she is energized by the felt connection between her adult teaching self and the potentially equally informed adult in her students. Because this is a relationship between equals, power is not an issue, and will yields to imagination. Such a teacher imagines—that is, *images*—the adult in her students, rather than their child-like or adolescent weaknesses.

I posit, then, a knowing adult within each student, and an unknowing, exploring child within the teacher, and good teaching is defined as whatever results from the connection of such a teacher with such students. Let us look more closely at how that connection is established.

## TRANSFERENCE/COUNTERTRANSFERENCE IN TEACHING

How do people connect with one another? Psychoanalysts have provided the most subtle and far-reaching answer to this question because they know, or have learned from hard and painful experience, that the relationship between themselves and their patients is the key to successful work. In this they differ from teachers, for whom the curriculum (the "subject") may seem to be a mediating factor, even though in fact (as we have seen) it is not. So here I draw on analytic theory in what follows. I do not mean to imply that teaching is the same as analysis, but there are nevertheless points of overlap. One is that *relationship* is the key to good teaching, too. Another is that a teacher—any teacher—is seen by students as a person invested with power, and, because where there is power there must be powerlessness, students feel some helplessness, especially at the beginning of a school year, when they are not yet sure what their teacher will be like. This relationship of power/powerlessness is felt at some level on both sides, together with feelings of knowledge/ignorance, order/chaos, independence/dependence—and age/youth.

These issues are not new for our students. They have faced them at home all their lives. Parents too have power, and use it. Each school year begins the working out of the relationship between teacher and student along such family lines. That is why there is so much tension, so much expectancy, at each beginning. If you remember any occasion when a parent found fault with you, you can feel how that experience is re-created in a student when a teacher hands him back a test paper. A test always carries with it the possibility of "getting caught." In both cases, the fear is the fear of not measuring up, or of being found unworthy or inadequate. Analysis and teaching both touch at such points, where familial tensions are re-created in the classroom.

The analyst's term for the means by which relationship is established, transference, has been defined as "the ubiquitous tendency to confuse the early figures in one's life with present ones" (Rodman 1986, 79–80). Early feelings about figures (especially parents) are transferred to another person in the here and now. This happens inevitably between teachers and students. In any classroom, conscious and unconscious relationships are created and maintained. As our students remind us of our past, so we represent for them adulthood. As they represent another chance for us to act like a parent, they see us as parental. As we connect with them, we are reminded of how we were treated at their age. If we like a student, it is probably because we have projected on to him a part of ourselves of which we are fond, so that the student seems familiar and comfortable to us. It is entirely unconscious but very real. The model of transference described here is based on Jung's "The Psychology of the Transference" (Jung 1977). In that work he deals with the archetypal underpinnings of the transference, and he makes an analogy, between transference and alchemical processes, which can seem arcane. Here I mean to make a more commonsense use of this word. I mean to depict with it what is *ordinarily* and *regularly* projected by student on to teacher, and vice versa, during teaching. Bear in mind always that projection is an unconscious process. We are here looking at something which goes on at all times, but which goes on "underneath" the observable events. Here we look at one reason why our memorable teachers stay memorable: They almost certainly filled some need we had that developed, probably, early in our growing up. We did not know what it was, but we nevertheless felt a sense of completion, of closure; of comfort; of excitement or challenge. Conversely, a teacher who made us feel anxious or angry was probably recalling some long-ago pain, now repressed, but reborn in the transference.

Adapting Jung's model, then, Figure 1 delineates the relationships between teacher and student. In this figure, "CS" means conscious, and "UCS" means unconscious. The beginning of the relationship is conscious, and is therefore represented by the line that links the conscious awareness of the teacher to the conscious awareness of the student: the top horizontal line (1) in the diagram. This line represents what each knows and sees about the other and is the site of the first stage of the relationship. The vertical arrows (3, 4) represent the relationship between the consciousness and the unconsciousness of teacher and student, re-

Figure 1
Conscious and Unconscious Relationships in Teaching

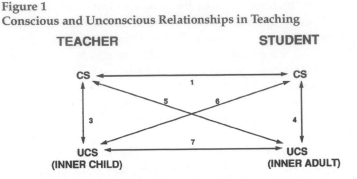

spectively. What is important here is that the teacher's inner child lives mostly in the teacher's unconscious, and the adult part of the student is similarly mostly unconscious. The genuine surprise teachers often feel when a class has gone exceptionally well is a measure of how unconscious the inner child is. Similarly, the student who writes something quite marvelous may wonder "where it came from" and be similarly surprised: It comes, often, from the student's inner, knowing adult. (The bottom line (7) is the unconscious relationship. Because it is by definition unknowable, it need not concern us here.)

Here are the steps in the developing relationship, over time, of teacher and student, when things go well. The introjection of teacher by students (5) sanctions the teacher's authority; the introjection of students by teacher (6) sanctions their youth, their unknowingness, and—above all—their energy.

This introjection of the student by the teacher determines the teacher's relationship to the student, the countertransference. What happens is that the student within the teacher is "fed" by actual students, and the teacher within the student is similarly nourished by the presence of the actual teacher, with the result that each feels what the other feels. Such a state is *empathy*.

The hope is that this empathy, once established, will continue throughout the school year, throughout the whole time the teacher is working with a particular student. But at some point, or rather at various points during the school year, if things have gone well, a final stage occurs: The student finds that her own inner teacher is all she needs. She can do the work *on her own*. And not just do-it-to-get-it-done. I mean doing it because the inner teacher is helping her with it. When this happens, the outer teacher is no longer needed. The crucial moment, and the measure of success, is that moment when the student says, "I knew that. I knew that all along." Thus we succeed only when we are no longer needed. To summarize: Good teaching is teaching driven by the teacher's unknowing, eager, inner child. This child makes a connection with students, who see that their teacher is somehow "like" them. Then they begin to feel the presence of their own inner teacher. Empathy results; and this leads, finally, to independence. As a child wants to show its parents, so a student will want to show the teacher, "I can do it myself." That is both the goal and the result of good teaching. The goal, in other words, is to render oneself useless, or at least, from the student's point of view, obsolete. Being content with this, being rewarded by this, is part of what teaching in the third stage is all about.

From a student's point of view a good teacher represents, to begin with, a person for whom individual and random events in the world and in personal life are subordinated to a larger, more orderly idea of the whole but who, at the same time, has a child-driven imagination and energy. Then, as the student's inner teacher is increasingly empowered, the real teacher fades in importance. That is what we mean when we say a student has "mastered" what we have taught. That is the place in this progression where teacher and student become equals. The recognition of such equality by the teacher is the moral center of teaching. It is the place where neither power nor subservience operates. Ideally, the student can now begin again—the next unit, the next year— with added confidence. Note *begin again*. The underlying pattern of teaching is the pattern of a journey in which "every end is a new beginning."

Let us look more closely at the transaction between the teacher's inner child and the student's inner adult. The relationship between the teacher and any student begins, of course, with the obvious inequalities: The teacher is older and is, in Lacan's phrase, "the one supposed to know." The student is younger and is supposed ignorant. But there is a more subtle and more important inequality. The healthy teacher's inner child is actually *more* eager, active, and exploring than is the real-life student. Most real-life students, especially those in high school, feel more or less obligated to present a "cool," uninvolved persona toward academic work and therefore toward most teachers as well. The constant effort to maintain this persona drains energy away from the more exploratory, more eager actual student. Anyone who has ever observed or taught in both junior and senior high schools has seen this process at work. Younger students are more open and more eager than older ones. But if the teacher's inner child is palpably present, it will actively "play" with the student-as-young-person, no matter what the age of the student. This meeting up results in a relationship of equals, or, to use the Jungian term, a *coniunctio*. The child-in-the-teacher and the actual young person begin to play with one another *as equals* for a short time. The teacher is as rewarded by the feeling of equality as the student is surprised by it. Ideally, they will both move to other such meetings, at higher cognitive and affective levels, as the year progresses. After this happens the student begins to care for the "fused" child; that is, the student takes on the role of mentor, guide, teacher. It is at this point that the student, by becoming a teacher, renders the actual teacher superfluous. A good way to imagine this process is to think of the teacher's inner child and the actual childlike student meeting up in the air, in the space above the two of them in the classroom. This is a space neither "in" the teacher nor "in" the student—that is, in neither of their conscious or unconscious minds. Rather, this is a process going on in a shared mutual space which belongs to both but of which both are typically unaware.

This is a hard concept for the purely rational mind. Here is a "preparatory," incomplete example. I am at this moment looking at the keyboard of my word processor. The keys are surely "there," and "real" for me. It is only by an effort of imagination that I can "image" the light that is reflected off them and which then travels through space on its way to my eyes; and yet it is this movement of the light in the space *between* the keys and my eyes that makes them "real" for me. But the mutual-space concept is even more subtle. Nathan Schwartz-Salant writes:

This space is a transitional area between the space-time world (where processes are characterized as an interaction of objects) and the collective unconscious—the *pleroma* (Jung 1952, par. 629). This area has a fundamentally different quality from the space-time world. In its pathological form, the pleroma invades the conscious personality as primary-process thinking. But in its creative form, it is the source of healing through one's experience of the *numinosum*. Images have the capacity to lead a person into the mystery of the pleroma. Marilyn Ferguson explains how T. S. Eliot's poems refer to the pleroma: "The still point of the turning world," she noted, "is neither flesh nor fleshless, neither arrest nor movement." Eliot wrote: "And do not call it fixity, where past and future are gathered. Except for the point, the still point / There would be no dance, and there is only the dance." . . . A new level of awareness has been reached when one has become conscious of the existence of this area. It is best not to identify this area with either implicate or space-time orders, but to allow it to be a connecting domain that cannot be cast in spatial categories. The third area is neither inside, outside, *nor* "in between" people. It is neither material nor psychic, "neither flesh nor fleshless," but is a realm of ethers. (Schwartz-Salant 1989, 107–8).

We don't attend to this in-between space, yet it is in this space that the relationship between teacher and student forms and grows. We must imagine it as inhabited by figures of the knowing adult and of the inner child: the attention-craving, the bored, the sleeping, the eager, the distracted—the whole imaginal world of the classroom. If we could ever see these figures we would feel we had fallen, like Alice, into another universe. But it would be a universe as real as Alice's encounters with the Mad Hatter and the Red Queen. The imaginal world of teaching is as rich and as strange, but, luckily for us, a bit less random and topsy-turvy. In the final chapter I shall look at this world as *liminal space*. Here, though, let us watch a few actual contests and meetings involving the inner child and the knowledgeable adult.

## THE UNKNOWING CHILD/KNOWING ADULT IN REAL CLASSROOMS

Ms. Shepley has a free period after the class I've just visited. This gives us a chance to go to the English department office and talk over what has transpired. I like to start by asking what the student has thought of things; specifically, how closely her estimate of what happened compares with what she wanted to happen—her ideal. We talk about what actually happened, and I ask what changes she might make in subsequent work with this group. Ms. Shepley saw (and felt) that her lecture about the phoenix was pretty much of a bomb. But, she says, she was in a dilemma: She wanted her students to know the material, and how else was she to "cover" it efficiently? Surely she can't ask them about something they've never heard of. I agree with her. "Covering" material is most efficiently done with "direct influence," in this case, lecturing. The question is whether the covering is worth the emotional cost. During the lecture students shuffled in their seats, looked down and around, played with pencils. One student braided the hair of the girl sitting in front of her. They were polite enough, but they just weren't really *there* with her, and Ms. Shepley knew it.

There is a paradox here. The more a teacher "needs" to cover something, the more the students tune out. Conversely, if a teacher seems utterly to be enjoying herself, with no outside pressure to cover some particular thing, attention focuses, energy is generated, and things go better. "Needing" or "having" to cover something is the purely adult side of the teacher, the side that does not, cannot, engage the student. It is pure will and no imagination, or at least very little. Especially with such a small number of students, the trick is to lecture in a very informal, low-key style. Ms. Shepley made too much of her presentation, saying things like "listen carefully now," and "you need to know about this." It is a common mistake for one just starting out, and certainly not a large-scale problem. Underneath the choice to lecture is the issue of a teacher's authority: when to use it, and when to let up. Ms. Shepley hasn't taught long enough to be really sure of her knowing adult, and lecturing is one way for her to shore up this figure in herself. So we talk about that, about authority and its uses. But doing so reminds me that I must now deal with authority in a different, less fun way: I have to go down and apologize to Mrs. Marvin, that assistant principal I didn't wait for, the one official in the office who can give a visitor a pass.

Mrs. Marvin is, alas, both available and upset. "We can't let people into the building without a pass," she says. I tell her I waited as long as I could. I don't tell her what I'm thinking: If it's her job to give out the passes then it's her job to be in the office to give them out, especially when school is starting for the day.

Instead I just listen and nod, and wait to see if she'll cool down. I know she's doing her thing, scolding me, but even so it makes me feel like a student myself, a student who has broken a rule. People in power in schools—administrators, where teachers are concerned, and teachers, where students are concerned—have many chances to make the people they work with feel either older (more competent, more knowledgeable) or younger (dumb, clumsy, or wrong) than they actually are. I notice that the younger I feel as Mrs. Marvin scolds me the angrier and more frustrated I get. That's going to lead to trouble if I show it, though, so I gear up my most mature teacher-doctor-therapist persona, and I try to watch the whole process from the outside, with a detached, clinical eye. I'm almost not hearing her. But I look at her attentively, I apologize again, and then it's OK for me to leave. I'm glad to get out of there and back to my real work. I've never had much use for administrators.

Nevertheless the split I felt, between child and adult is, as I have said, crucial for what makes teaching work. Mrs. Marvin reminded me, by making it feel guilty, that there is a child inside me. And it is this inner child—in its livelier moments—that has everything to do with good teaching. Ms. Shepley's easy and natural connection with her students flows from her inner child too: They sense in her the fun, the engagement, that her child brings to the work. It is what will make her a good teacher.

Another example, this one from my own beginning. One of my classes in my first teaching experience at Natick, was, as I've said, a zoo. It was the lowest, or "general," track, and they were tenth graders. Once, though, and only because I hadn't planned anything else, I asked them to write a paragraph about the brand-new, all glass-and-chrome high school that had just been opened that very September. I assumed they loved it. It turned out they hated it, and missed the old, yellowed-brick pile that was now the junior high. I was astonished, and asked them to write more. They did. Then I asked them how they'd redesign the new school. They did that, complete with drawings and plans. For a week things went very well, and I was learning something about these students and about how to connect. The reason these students hated the new building was that they didn't feel a part of the high school anyway: They were never encouraged to go out for teams or the pom-pom squad, so they hung out solely with one another. In the old building they could do this in the basement, or in empty classrooms, or in an unused storage space. Here, in this flashy, zippy, modern place, there was no place to hide. We talked seriously about this issue. But then they got antsy: "When are we going to get back to English?" they asked, meaning grammar. What we were doing was interesting and unusual, but it wasn't school, in their view. If I'd had more experience I would have stayed with it, but I thought they were probably right, and anyway I knew Miss Greene would prefer the grammar too. So I capitulated and the zoo returned. But for a few days there the child in me took over, and I was having fun as well as learning some important things about my very unfamiliar students. I was able to feel a connection because my students were educating me; they were the adults. My imagination was stimulated by what they were doing. It was a reversal of the ordinary roles, though. Teaching is not supposed to be driven by imagination and connection; rather, it is usually seen to be a matter of power (in the teacher) and subservience (on the part of students), especially if the students are less than gifted. Again, will vs. imagination. Let me supply one more example from that first year in teaching.

One day, as part of the teacher preparation program in which I was enrolled, my methods teacher addressed all of us on the subject of discipline. At some time, he told us, we might have to discipline a student whose name we did not know: in the lunch room, for example. In this case, he said, the thing to do was to go up to the student and ask, severely, "What's your name?" This, he assured us, would melt any student, rendering him, or her, compliant instantly. And indeed, some months later, there I was, doing lunch room duty, when I saw a boy throw a milk carton. Summoning as much severity as I could, I went over to him and demanded, "What's your name?"

"What's it to you?" he replied.

My methods teacher hadn't said this could occur. But here he was, looking up at me, and here were his friends, waiting to see what would happen. I had to do something, clearly. Without thinking—that is, without thinking consciously—I said, "Well, what's it to *you*?"

"Huh?" he said.

"What's it to you?" I repeated. "Your name. What's it to you? Does it matter what your name is?"

"Huh?"

"Well, look," I said. "I guess it doesn't matter to you what your name is, so I'll call you Murgatroyd. Now, Murgatroyd, how about going over and picking up that milk carton?"

His friends around the table couldn't resist. "C'mon, Murgatroyd," they said, and up he got, and I was off the hook. And very relieved.

Let us look at what happened here. When I first saw the boy throw the milk carton, I remembered what my (now internalized and idealized) methods teacher had said to do. I was, in effect, trying to "borrow" some of his authority and experience. I was hoping to act as a total adult, an authoritarian keeper of order. This I tried to do and I failed, miserably. I have no doubt that my methods teacher would have made it work. And note the power of my idealizing transference to him at the time! I was so unsure of my own adult authority that I tried to use his. Of course it didn't work. In this opening moment of our confrontation, then, there is in the space between me and this student a failing adult. From the student's point of view an actual failing adult (me) represents a prime target for his as yet unactualized but nevertheless very important (to him) adult side. So his inner (confident, even cocky) adult takes on my faltering adult, and says, "What's it to you?"

At this point my adult concedes defeat, and flees. Luckily my inner child is still there with me, and it is he who repeats the student's question back to him: "What's it to *you*?" My inner child is now having fun with the student's adult self; he is thinking something like "Bet he never thought of *that* question before." This makes me feel better at once; in the space between us, my inner child and the student's adult self are moving closer together, where they can negotiate. My inner child will kid the "adult" in the student until the student agrees to play my child's game; that is, he will agree to "become" Murgatroyd when my child makes that suggestion. (To this day, thirty-four years later, I have no idea where the name "Murgatroyd" came from.) Now, when the student enters the game, he and I are equals and we play together for an instant. Then he gets up from the table, *as Murgatroyd* (so his "adult" persona isn't damaged), and goes over to get the milk carton. As he does so he is caring for the Murgatroyd-child in him, recognizing that it needs his help to become responsible and sensible—at least so it won't throw milk cartons when a teacher is looking. In caring for his own child he may only be urging it to be alert, but he may also be learning about responsibility, about growing up.

Of course I had no idea of any of this at the time. In my work as an analyst I am often aware of such matters, of all the "other people" who come into the room as I sit with a patient. These "people" are there in the classroom, too, but since each student creates her or his own constellation of them, the population of such imaginal figures in any given class is unimaginably diverse. Fortunately there are certain figures we will always find just because we are dealing with adolescents. The teacher connects with all of them primarily, as Guggenbuhl-Craig says, through the unknowing child/knowing adult archetype. Teaching deals above all with what is *new*; that is, new to students. Being on the edge of the unknown generates figures who are eager to explore and other figures who hesitate and draw themselves inward or pull themselves away from the abyss. These are the figures that populate the "realm of ethers," the pleroma of the classroom. How the child and the adult, the two poles of the teacher's archetype, relate to these figures will determine the success of the teaching. That success comes, as I have said, when the student no longer needs us, when there is equality between our own imaginal figures and those of our student. When this happens the student is now less alone on the journey. It has been our privilege as teachers to guide. We know the journey because we have traveled it ourselves. It is not just knowledge we purvey, but knowledge of the journey.

The journey—the great, universal journey, as Campbell (1949) reminds us—has four phases: Creation, Loss of Paradise, the Emergence of the Hero, and the Eternal Return. Creation, in teaching, is what happens at the beginning of any new piece of work. Where there was nothing, now something begins, as students begin reading the poem or play, begin a new form of writing, begin anything. The teacher has been through it, of course; but artful teaching, at this stage, demands that the teacher's knowledge be masked enough so that students will not be intimidated by it, and yet not so hidden that they will feel abandoned without a guide.

Loss of Paradise in teaching is easy to identify: It is that moment when the student finds out that the work will be harder than she thought, and it is that moment when the teacher finds she is having more than usual difficulty with this student, or with that class. The trauma implicit in reading, and then handing back, the first set of compositions in a new school year has often been remarked upon. This is loss of paradise for sure. But out of this comes the necessity for gearing up and getting into the task: The hero emerges, on both sides of the desk. The teacher begins to make connections and the students begin to see them, and both feel strengthened, invigorated.

The Eternal Return is the sacrifice of the hero's role to a greater one, the role of the person at home in the world as it is, no longer on the quest and therefore no longer at risk. The return celebrates and initiates a new state of order, harmony, and peace. For us and for our students it is the state of having mastered something. It is not a state that lasts, though, because there is always something new to master, as there is for Tennyson's Ulysses:

> All experience is an arch wherethro'
> Gleams that untravell'd world whose margin fades
> For ever and for ever when I move. (167)

Thus the cycle begins again with a new Creation at the next higher level, as our students grow, and as we teachers find newness in ourselves. One of the great gifts teaching gives us is the privilege of sharing our own journey with those who are given into our care. Not for us, thankfully, is what Auden called "the necessary impersonal life." This alone is cause for happy reflection, perhaps even celebration. The source of good teaching—connection to the child within us—is simultaneously the source of our reward, because our reward *is* connection, to our students and to our own inner selves.

## WORKS CITED

Campbell, Joseph. *The Hero with a Thousand Faces*. Princeton, New Jersey: Princeton University Press, 1949.

Ferguson, Marilyn. *The Holographic Paradigm*. Ed. Ken Wilbur. Boulder, Colorado: Shambhala Press, 1982.

Guggenbuhl-Craig, Adolf. *Power in the Helping Professions*. Dallas: Spring Publications, 1979.

Jung, C. G. "The Development of Personality." *The Development of Personality*. Vol. 17 of *The Collected Works of C. G. Jung*. 20 vols. Princeton, New Jersey: Bollingen Series XX, Princeton University Press, 1954.

————. "The Psychology of the Transference." *The Practice of Psychotherapy*. Vol. 16 of *The Collected Works of C. G. Jung*. 20 vols. Princeton, New Jersey: Bollingen Series XX, Princeton University Press, 1977.

McClelland, David C., et al. *The Achieving Society*. New York: Appleton-Century-Crofts, 1953.

Rodman, F. Robert. *Keeping Hope Alive*. New York: Harper and Row, 1986.

Schwartz-Salant, Nathan. *The Borderline Personality in Analysis: Vision and Healing*. Wilmette, Illinois: Chiron Press, 1989.

Tennyson, Alfred Lord. *The Poems and Plays of Alfred Lord Tennyson*. New York: Random House, 1938.

# Chapter Four

# Story

*Miranda*:    Your tale, sir, would cure deafness.
—*The Tempest*, Act 1, Scene 2

For many of us who teach English, the experience that drew us to this work in the first place was finding ourselves unexpectedly mirrored in a story. A child's world without stories in it would be nothing more than a stream of disparate and puzzling events. Add story, and we are at once given not a stream of random events but a place, so to speak, where the same things happen over and over again with reassuring consistency. Even horrible things can somehow be borne if we know how things will "come out in the end." The first *Babar* book begins, for example, with the killing of Babar's mother by a hunter; but if we know the story we know that eventually Babar will escape his captors and be taken care of by the kindly old lady—the mother of mothers—just as we would hope to be, should such a catastrophe befall us. This theme of abandonment, of being lost and found, is a part of the life, and the fear, of every child. When, grown older, we have such an encounter with story in a classroom, and when that encounter illuminates a similarly unknown or dark part of ourselves, we are not likely to forget. The debt of gratitude we owe that teacher can be, and surely in many cases has been, paid off when we followed her into the profession.

It is a wonderful moment when a student discovers that what is being read in class is "about *me*!" Teachers often talk about this as a goal, but stop short of sharing their own experience of journey. It is not the content of the journey that matters, but the doing of it. We must, together with our students, honor our own journey. I use, as illustrations for this process, first a way of planning to teach Willa Cather's "Paul's Case," and next a way of reading William Wordsworth's famed "Intimations" Ode.

I have found that for me planning the teaching of a piece of literature must begin with my own response to that literature; I then work with that response to develop my lesson plans. My planning does not begin with ideas about students, or literary criticism, or method. I believe, in short, that good planning begins in autobiography, not in pedagogy.

Pedagogy is the study of what teachers do. It is thus a study of the exercise of power. It defeats real learning because it presumes that students are in a secondary position. The sort of teaching I want to describe here begins not with knowledge, but with personal reflection begun in the teacher and continued in the student; its goal is equality of teacher with student, an equality conferred by occupying shared imaginal space. Thus my planning begins with where I was in my life when I did not know "English" as a field—as my students do not. What I seek to do is to return to and retrace the steps by which any one part of the field—in this instance, "Paul's Case"—came to have meaning for me. Having done that, I then design lessons which mirror my past process for my present students. My teaching thus becomes the mirror image of my learning. My planning begins with the question, "how did I learn, or come to believe, this?" The next step is to take students down that same path. Thus the question, "how shall I teach this?" is not well asked. "How did I learn this?" is the right starting point. The image of the mirror is important. We know our goal—a personal involvement of our students with our subject—because we have such an involvement ourselves. We therefore look back at when we began to achieve this, and when we see ourselves as unknowing, we see our students: another mirror. We work back in our own lives to where our involvement began, and we start there to begin a similar involvement in our students. We then work the class along until its involvement somehow resembles, at least in part, our own present relationship to the work. As teachers we must begin with the question of what it was like not to own the story, and then to have experienced it.

There is, I know, the view that we should *not* use our own involvement with the literature as a guide for planning because our own experience is too personal and likely to get in our students' way. I would answer this in two ways: (1) We owe it to our students to serve as role models for what involvement with literature does, and (2) Leaving students "alone" to respond is utopian: How can we know they have done so? Leaving them alone lets us fall all too easily into the "no-lose" position in teaching: If the students respond it's because we taught well, and if they don't, it's because they're dumb. Thus we empower ourselves without taking any responsibility for failure. We must, I feel, risk a more personal investment.

On to "Paul's Case." There must have been something in it with which I was already involved, consciously or not, because I was certainly moved by the story when I first read it in high school: not only moved, but scared. So my first task in planning is to try, as best I can, to find out what that something was. To argue from general principles such as, say, the primacy of plot, character, and setting, or theories of genre, or the life of the author, is to argue for ways of explaining involvement, rather than experiencing the involvement itself. For Aristotle, the experience of tragedy was the catharsis of pity and terror: That was the involvement. I am interested here in the experience itself, and indeed I feel pity and terror as I read this story.

My first reading of "Paul's Case" took place when I was in the tenth grade. The story both fascinated and frightened me. I read and reread it that year and have done so since, for thirty-six years. I am struck by the extent to which I identify with Paul. I do not remember any scene in my life comparable to the one with which the story opens, where Paul must face the accusations of his teachers; but I do know that I had a fear that I would get caught at *something*, that I would be "found out," not because I did wicked things, but rather because no one paid much attention to anything

I did, most of the time. Not that I was neglected: It was just that I was a very introverted only child, and so absorbed with my mineral collection and my microscope that I was left alone by my parents a good deal. Thus I never quite knew where I stood with them, and because I wouldn't have thought of asking, I spent a lot of time wondering "what would happen if I . . .," and since I knew other people got into trouble sometimes, I wondered a lot about what it would be like. So I learned a lot from that opening scene when I was in the tenth grade. But what the teachers do doesn't "work" in the story. Paul ignores their assault. I didn't think I'd be able to do that, and I both envied him and felt vaguely guilty for doing so.

Next, Paul enters a series of private worlds, reveries: in the painting gallery, and at the concert. I did a good deal of that, too. Fortunately for me, though, the space between reverie and reality was not nearly so wide for me as it is for Paul: I did not have to walk back, through the rain, to Cordelia Street, to a dreadful house and a trapped, hostile father. Nevertheless I could feel how alone Paul is.

Paul's flight from the real Pittsburgh to the romantic New York had special meaning for me too. I lived in New Jersey as a child and I often drove, with my mother, from our farm there to visit my grandparents in New York City. I liked the farm and I was used to it; New York, by contrast, was full of people and strange noises that never let up, even at night: Lying in my bed I could hear car horns and sirens and the screech of the Third Avenue elevated trains, a vibrant concatenation that was completely different from nights at the farm, their silence interrupted only by sounds of a cat or an owl.

Part of that trip to New York involved driving through Hoboken and then over the Jersey meadows on the Pulaski Skyway. The meadows were then, and still are, a dismal wasteland of industrial litter, and Hoboken was an ominous clutter of rows of similar houses, telephone poles with hundreds of wires strung on them, and crowds of unfamiliar people. I was frightened driving through these streets; I feared being abandoned there, although I never let on. Hoboken was the world of the frighteningly ordinary for me, just as Cordelia Street was for Paul.

Finally, his dream played out, Paul kills himself, in those very New Jersey meadows which I knew. "The picture making mechanism was crushed, the disturbing visions flashed into black, and Paul dropped back into the immense design of things" (121). Was that, then, death? A blank? No pictures, only black? I had faced that question before, in two ways. One was through an early childhood fascination with Egypt. I was especially interested in mummies and, by extension, in the Egyptian idea of the afterlife. They thought that the afterlife was—if you got there—pretty much the same as life here: a house, a pond, trees, your family around; and their well-stocked tombs provided for this next life. I liked that a lot better than some nebulous heaven, or some idea of being just a soul, which seemed to me too much like being a ghost. I was fascinated by ghosts, too, but I didn't want to be one. Cather's description of Paul's afterlife was the more mesmerizing for being so explicit, and the more frightening for being so hopeless.

The other way I thought about death as a young child was through a Hogarth engraving. My parents had an enormous (to me) bound collection of Hogarth prints, at which I looked from time to time, on my own. It had a number of pictures in it that interested me, especially pictures of firemen squirting feeble streams of water from hand-powered pumpers at huge London conflagrations. But the print that fascinated and scared me above all was one of an anatomy dissection, in which an elegant teacher gestures at a cadaver while he explains something to a group of students gathered around the table. The cadaver's head is penetrated by a large hook; a rope rises from this hook to a pulley in the ceiling, far above, and returns, enabling the teacher to raise the head by pulling on the rope. The entrails of the body spill out of it, and the heart, which has rolled on to the floor, is being eaten by a dog. I used to thumb through the book, knowing where this picture was, half hoping it would be gone; but it was always there, and I almost always ended up looking at it. My feeling about "Paul's Case" today is exactly like my feeling about the Hogarth print then. I am frightened still, but I am nevertheless drawn to read, and reread.

My planning, then, starts with this mixture of fright and fascination, brought on by some combination of death and otherness. I hope it is clear that while the circumstances that gave rise to these feelings in me are undoubtedly unique, the feelings themselves— fear and fascination—are not. For me, then, this story and its hero are not pathological or exotic. Instead, they are strangely, threateningly familiar. To plan, I need to uncover what it is in me that makes this so.

Willa Cather gave a curious title to the collection of stories in which "Paul's Case" was included: *The Troll Garden*. Rosowski (1986) says this of the title:

Cather's central metaphor reveals much. She wrote of art made by trolls or hawked by goblins to lure innocents away from human existence. The point of view in each of these stories is that of the ordinary person outside the garden who glimpses the troll magic or hears stories of it, but, because unable to create it, is distrustful. For such persons art is painful or threatening. (29)

The feeling, then, is this: there is something wonderful that I can neither do nor have. This feeling I recognize in myself, and so this idea provides me a place to begin my lesson planning. Before looking at the story at all, I ask students to write about such subjects as: Where would you be if you did not have to be here? Is there a place to which you would like to go, but from which you feel shut out? If so, where is it? What would you do there? If not, was there such a place at one time in your life, and how did you manage to enter it? For students who genuinely feel no such place, I might suggest some: the world of a travel magazine or a Christmas department store window, or perhaps the world in a painting chosen by the student from a pile of reproductions.

Responding to such writing means, in essence, entering into the student's world along with the student. My comments on the paper may ask further questions, or may wonder about further possibilities in this "other" world. Since we cannot know, rationally, what the student's imagined world is like in all particulars, we must ask questions, as a child would.

The idea of *other* is now visible in the class. So far, though, it is a more attractive, more romantic other. There must also be, of course, the necessary reverse of this, the frightening, *ordinary* other. For Paul, this is Cordelia Street. "[Paul] is forever separated from the glittering world he seeks to enter, yet just as separated from the common world he seeks to leave" (Rosowski 1986, 28). What is so frightening here is that he is lost entirely: He has no place to go. He "loses himself" in his reveries before the paintings, and among his flowers and silks in his New York hotel room; but these are somnambulistic states, withdrawals from the world; they are not real places; they are not life. Life, for Paul, contains fear, and so he cannot "choose life." He cannot connect with other people: not the English teacher, the drawing master, the "sympathetic" principal, his father, the actors, the Yale undergraduate. Because he has never connected with anyone he feels he has no choices to make about the world outside: It simply will not have him. Compare Hamlet, who asserts that our fear of death "makes us rather bear those ills we have / Than fly to others that we know not of." This is precisely what Paul cannot do: He cannot bear his present ills, and his fear of death is by no means so strong. It is, for him, the only remaining option, the only available choice, and he takes it. Thus our next task is to face, with our class, the feeling of having no choice, nowhere to go.

Recall that our first assignment had to do with positive choice. We asked, in effect, "If not now, when? If not here, where? If not this, what?" Now we must ask, When—if ever—have you felt that you had no other alternatives, that is, no choice?

Here is a variant of the *Steppingstones* exercise (Progoff 1975). Each of us creates, in class but privately, a graph that represents the high and low points of our life so far. Starting with birth, we simply draw a line to represent the course of our life: It goes up when things were going well, and down when they weren't. My experience has been that we all create lines that flow up and down radically, dramatically. I've never seen a chart that just went flatly along, or contained only gentle undulations. The charts of a group of eighth graders whom I taught a few years ago had as many oscillations in them as mine does; age and experience don't increase the amplitude of the rising and falling or the number of ups and downs. Next we write, privately or in a journal, an account of one of the "down" times. Almost always such an account turns out to be a time in our lives when we felt isolated, cut off, and without others who would understand us and help us. We felt, in short, like Paul.

With these two pieces of writing accomplished—and note that we have done them along with our students—we are in a good position to begin our reading of "Paul's Case." The writing has explicated in our own lives the poles of Paul's experience: the romantic yearning for Other, and the fear of the common, or of being lost. Our work as a teacher is to create these situations in which our students can, and do, see themselves. We do not leave to chance the possibility of students making idiosyncratic connections with the story. Instead, we look for some shared space, that is, the imaginal space shared by us with our students. I found this space by first exploring the connections the story has with my life, and I then designed activities which re-created in my students inner, psychological situations in which I have found myself. These connections between my students and myself stay in my mind throughout the teaching of "Paul's Case."

We may think, then, of the teaching of literature as involving three overlapping, and therefore potentially shareable, fields: our experience, the experience of our students, and the experience of (and therefore in) the text. Exclude any one, and our success will be left to chance. All too often, though, the text alone is the only subject in the class and, when that is so, chance or luck is all that remains to help us in our task.

I want to end with some theoretical underpinning for this approach. I do this for two reasons: because the theory interests me, but also to proceed in a more traditional way for a moment, in order to illustrate what the power—the authority—of theory feels like. Here is a quotation from *The Responsive Chord* (Schwartz, 1974). I have interpolated, in brackets, observations of my own which apply his thesis directly to teaching:

A listener or viewer brings far more to the communication event than a communicator can put into his program, commercial, or message. [Students know, or have experienced, far more than what can be formally taught.] The communicator's problem, then, is not to get stimuli across, or even to package his stimuli so that they can be understood and absorbed. Rather, he must deeply understand the kinds of information and experiences stored in his audience, the patterning of this information, and the interactive process whereby stimuli evoke this stored information. (21)

The teacher's problem, in short, is not to design understandable or absorbable material. The teacher's task is to evoke in her students what is already stored in them, usually in some unacknowledged or unconscious way.

Schwartz's term for this idea is the "resonance principle." His basic point is that successful communication depends on resonance between what is already owned by an audience and what is being newly presented to it. I cannot emphasize too strongly that the resonance principle is a direct challenge to the conventional assumption on which teaching is supposed to be based: that teachers are to teach material which is new to the student. In contrast, the resonance principle stresses the point that successful communication depends on what is already shared between communicator and respondent. Successful teaching finds this common ground. This common ground must develop in the students, consciously or unconsciously, as the teaching proceeds, or else resonance never occurs and students stay alienated from what they are reading. As teachers of English, we are the exemplars of the effects of resonance.[1]

Another source of theory is myth. Apollo, god of schools and clarity and thought, gave the ancient Greeks, and us, three principles that can guide our teaching lives. First, *moderation in all things*: Never be one-sided; don't pursue order at the expense of spontaneity, or correctness at the expense of expression, or freedom at the expense of structure. Second, *honor the gods*: There are ideas and feelings in what we do that are more than we can know; we deal with life and death, change and growth, and life's journey. Be reverent in the face of these things, but welcome them joyfully. Finally, *know thyself*, which is, of course, the argument of this chapter. For the source of what we do is not in books or students, but in ourselves. The paradox of teaching is that we honor our students best when we honor who *we* are—our own individual and idiosyncratic selves.

So much for theory. Now, back to what we try to do. The risk we must take is that of being ourselves in our classrooms. We cannot stand aside, hoping that pedagogy and the story will work on their own. Our lives must be caught up in the very stuff of the story, the poem, the play. The question is not, "How shall I teach 'Paul's Case'?" Rather, the question is, "Where is 'Paul's Case' in me?" I have given you my answer, but I cannot give you yours: That will come from your story within. All I can do is urge you to bring that question, and your answer, into your classroom. Then all will be well. Our deepest and richest teaching forms in our own heart's core.

With this as a guiding principle, I will look at a story of reconnection to the child archetype discussed in the previous chapter, and seen there as the source of energy for teaching as it connects us with the inner adult in our students. The "story" I have chosen is a story about the archetypal child: Wordsworth's "Ode: Intimations of Immortality from Recollections of Early Childhood." But first I want to amplify the concept of *imaginal space*.

By imaginal space I mean the space, including the images and feelings and people and memories it contains, that we create around ourselves when we reflect on who we are and how we became what we are. Our imaginal space combines the "now" of our life together with our images of our life's journey to this point. In addition, imaginal space can include images and questions that arise from our speculations about where our life is leading us. Our awareness of our own imaginal space is not constant; usually, in fact, we are too enmeshed in the daily round of the events of our lives ("distracted from distraction by distraction,"—T. S. Eliot) to allow ourselves to become aware of our imaginal space. Instead, our awareness of it comes upon us unexpectedly and, because reflection is not something we are used to, the experience is sometimes painful.

The planning for "Paul's Case" is one example of how a reflection into our imaginal space might begin. But reflection can be more positive, of course, as it is in the Wordsworth poem that is discussed below. As we shall see, the poem may be read as a description, over time, of the poet's experience of his own imaginal space.

The second dimension of imaginal space is the space described in, and embodied by, a work of literature. Aristotle asserted that the means by which literature creates imaginal space are plot, character, thought, diction, spectacle, and melody. These "means" have their effects on the reader, but even when no reader is present they are, so to speak, lying in wait for a reader to come along.

This is the point at which the content of the work touches the archetypal ground.

We have, then, imaginal space in the work, and imaginal space in the reader. When we consider the teaching of literature, we must add a third element: the interaction of the imaginal space of the teacher with the imaginal space of the student. Obviously it is partly through the agency of the teacher that the work is brought to the student. Equally obviously, the teacher's imaginal space differs significantly from that of a student. As teachers know all too well, their age, experience, and enthusiasm often seem to create more problems than they solve when teaching is being done. The perennial student reactions to a book—"This is boring," or, "Why do we have to read this?"—are not just reactions to the book. They are also challenges to the teacher's authority and wisdom. And teachers often respond defensively: "You may not like this now, but someday. . . ." Someday, the teacher might just as well be saying, you will be as wise as I am, but for now you're unformed, ignorant, and unworthy. I know this and you don't. So there. Obviously these "challenging" responses by students undercut such a teacher at every step, and such responses by the teacher serve only to further separate teacher and student. There is no shared ground between them, only difference—of age and status and experience and knowledge. Both teacher and student are involved in a question of who can win. The student's flip, casual persona is summoned into the classroom to do battle with the teacher's stuffy adulthood. This contest has very little to do with teaching unless the teacher can make genuine use of it, a very difficult thing to do. In general it is better not to get into the problem in the first place. What we are after is shared ground, not a turf war.

What we are after, in part, is a positive transference, to return to that earlier conceptualization. If, at the unconscious-to-unconscious level of the transference/countertransference diagram (the bottom line, see Figure 1), there can be a communication of my fear with a congruent unconscious fear in the student, we will be on our way. ("Unconscious fear" is oxymoronic: It would be more accurate to say, "repressed fear." But fear it is, nevertheless.)

What we are doing here is meeting the student's more or less automatic, persona-driven "I don't get this," or "Why do we have to read this?" with a counterargument: If you read this, something will happen in your life, something unpredictable, something only you can find out, because a something happened in me, *and I didn't expect anything either.*

If we conceptualize imaginal space in the following way, we can see the theory, at least, of how this is a solution to this problem of the unwilling reader; we can see the shared ground of the unexpected. Imagine the three domains of imaginal space as depicted in Figure 2.

We see from this figure that there is a space where the three imaginal spaces coincide: where the teacher, the student, and the work join in *equal* partnership. It is at this point, and only at this point, that significant teaching can be done. To teach from the teacher's experience is to make the real agenda the teacher's need for power: I know and you don't. To teach from the writer's experience is an exercise in scholarship (at best), although at the secondary level it is usually a covert expression of that same need

**Figure 2**
**Imaginal Space**

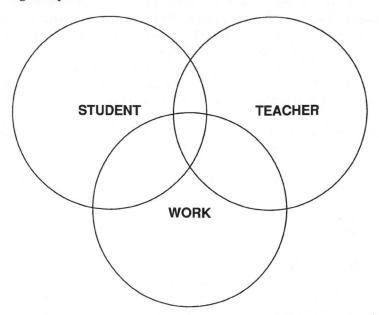

STUDENT    TEACHER

WORK

for power: You can't understand this work unless you know all these historical or biographical facts.

I propose now to undertake an exploration of Wordsworth's "Intimations" Ode to provide another illustration of how teaching in the shared imaginal space can be done. Over and over again in reading Wordsworth we enter with him into a world of reminiscence, where a past state is recalled as magical and wonderful, while the present is flat and dull:

> Heaven lies about us in our infancy———
> Shades of the prison-house begin to close
>     Upon the growing boy,
> But he beholds the light, and whence it flows,
>     He sees it in his joy;
> The youth, who daily farther from the east
>     Must travel, still is Natures's priest,
>     And by the vision splendid
>     Is on his way attended;
> At length the man perceives it die away
> And fade into the light of common day. (lines 66–76)

This passage is written about "us," that is, all of us. But is it necessarily so? Must our connection to light, or nature, or heaven dissolve as we grow up? Is this the inevitable result of the inexorable passage of days and years? Are we, now, as adults, condemned to live only in "the light of common day"? To ask this question another way, must we lose the child in us as we grow up?

My thesis is that what lies beneath the Ode is the loss and then the recovery, as Wordsworth experienced it, of the child in him; that the loss is not as inevitable as Wordsworth claims, but that when the child is lost, the consequences are serious for anyone. I will describe a method by which we may get in touch with this experience of loss and recovery of the child in ourselves. The inner child is of particular importance for teachers, as we have seen. But in one sense we are all teachers: Whether we teach others or not, we continually teach ourselves. Within each of us there is both a knowing adult and an unknowing child. For example, your first experience of a new place (your hotel room on a vacation, say) is often the experience of an eager, curious child. Does water come out of the tap? There's a big tree outside our window! That sort of thing. So when I speak of teaching I mean an inner dialogue we may have with ourselves whenever the child and the adult in us talk, playfully or seriously, across the years of our lives. We, all of us, have much to learn from experiencing, vicariously, Wordsworth's loss of "the glory and the freshness of a dream," and his working toward restoration and renewal. We must, I believe, look into ourselves as Wordsworth so consistently did; and we must look, as he did, for the inner child. For all of us (but especially for teachers, as we have seen), the inner child is a source of energy, playfulness, and fun, as well as providing a challenge to the adult in our students. Furthermore, because it can feel earth as mother, it is connected to the natural world in wonderful and sometimes frightening ways. This connection is, over and over, a theme for Wordsworth.

The inner child is also to a greater or lesser extent the archetypal child. "Archetypal" is a word now in fairly common use, but, as so often happens, its meaning has become fuzzy as a result. Although Jung did not invent the term, it was he who gave it its modern significance, and I want now to sketch briefly the history of Jung's idea of archetypes, with emphasis on the child archetype.

Jung was Freud's most important disciple for roughly seven years. Freud's unimaginably courageous discovery, in himself, of repressed sexuality in infancy and childhood was literally epoch-making. It was nothing less than the discovery of the unconscious. For Freud, the unconscious is created when we, in earliest infancy and later, repress drives and wishes that are too terrifying to remain conscious: the drive to possess the parent of the opposite sex, the drive to kill the rival, same-sex parent; these wishes, repressed, become the contents of the unconscious, and are later expressed in symbolic form in dreams and symptoms. (We now know that they are also, tragically, acted out in real life.) For Freud, the unconscious is created anew in each new child as the Oedipal drama is replayed in each family. Freud saw Jung as his "son and heir" in psychoanalysis, the person best suited to carry forward the theory that the unconscious is made up solely of the repressed sexual and aggressive instincts, what Freud called the "id," the animal nature of the child and of all of us. But in 1912, as we have seen, the relationship between Jung and Freud came to an end because, in that year, Jung published *Wandlungen und Symbole der Libido*, later translated into English as *Psychology of the Unconscious* and now known as *Symbols of Transformation* (Jung 1956). There Jung argued for the first time that the unconscious is not solely created out of the family triangle, that it is not just instinctual in origin, but that it has another, transpersonal, aspect as well, a dimension that transcends individual and family experience, but that is nevertheless an innate part of all human nature. He asserted that there are "organizing factors," the archetypes, which are to be understood as inborn modes of functioning that constitute, in their totality, man's nature. "The chick does not learn how to come out of the egg—it possesses this knowledge *a priori*" (par. 505). In a key passage, Jung challenged the Freudian theory head on:

Religious and conventional morality join forces with Freudian theory in consistently devaluing the regression [the wish to return to the mother] and its ostensible goal—reversion to infantilism—as "infantile sexuality," "incest," "uterine fantasy," etc.... [T]herapy must support the regression, and continue to do so until the "prenatal" stage is reached. It must be remembered that the "mother" is really an imago, a psychic image merely, which has a number of different but very important unconscious contents. The "mother," as the first incarnation of the anima archetype [that is, of the unconscious feminine in the male] personifies in fact the whole unconscious. Hence the regression leads back only apparently to the mother; in reality she is the gateway to the unconscious, to the "realm of the Mothers." Whoever sets foot in this realm submits his conscious ego-personality to the controlling influence of the unconscious. ... [R]egression, if left undisturbed, does not stop short at the "mother" but goes beyond her to the prenatal realm of the "Eternal Feminine," to the immemorial world of archetypal possibilities where, "thronged round with images of all creation," slumbers the "divine child," patiently awaiting his conscious realization. This son is the germ of wholeness. . . . It is these inherent possibilities of "spiritual" or "symbolic" life and of progress which form the ultimate, if unconscious, goal of regression. (par. 507–10)

In other words, it is not union with the personal mother which we seek, as Freud asserted; rather, it is a reconnection to creation itself, to origins—to the archetypes.

Here Jung and Wordsworth intuit together the realm of the archetypes:

> Our birth is but a sleep and a forgetting:
> The soul that rises with us, our life's star,
>     Hath had elsewhere its setting
>     And cometh from afar.
>     Not in entire forgetfulness,
>     And not in utter nakedness,
> But trailing clouds of glory do we come
>     From God who is our home. (lines 57–65)

As Jung (1970, par. 728) said, "Man brings with him at birth the ground-plan of his nature." Jung and Wordsworth both assert that we come into the world bringing something with us. It is Freud who insists we are born in utter nakedness, subject to primal instincts. For Jung we come trailing clouds of glory: our connections to the archetypes, our inborn patterns, our life's star. The infant for Jung is dependent, but also magical; human, but also divine. And not only this. The goal, Jung says, of the search for the eternal feminine, the return to nature, earth, and origins, leads to "the realm of the archetypes," and they, in turn, represent the "inherent possibilities of 'spiritual' or 'symbolic' life."

As with Jung, so with Wordsworth; each sees the deep meaning in return. It is no wonder that in nature Wordsworth sees both spirit and symbol. For most of us, our personal parents originally had the numinosity of god and goddess, and only gradually, as we took on their ways by growing up, did they lose for us their archetypal power. But Wordsworth is something like an orphan, his parents having died when he was so young. People without their actual parents often develop a hole in the psyche, through which the archetypal parents reach to them directly. For example, Jesus does not have a personal father and so readily and naturally comes to know instead his "father in heaven." Let us look at parent, nature, and archetype together, as Wordsworth may have done.

The concept of the archetype is hard to talk about because with it we enter the realm of the unconscious and so face an immediate paradox. If I lecture with Apollonian clarity and you listen with Dionysian eros-driven attentiveness, absolute understanding will prevail on all sides. We shall all feel illuminated. In other words, we shall all be absolutely conscious of everything that has transpired. This is the Apollonian ideal of education: illumination, "seeing the light," as we say, meaning purely conscious understanding. The dark unconscious is usually given no place in the world of lectures and seminars, and yet it is the ground and locus of my entire argument. The paradox is that we cannot make the unconscious conscious by talking about it. It will shift its ground, like the ghost of Hamlet's father under the floorboards; or it will reappear in unfamiliar forms and shapes, as Prospero has Ariel do. Above all remember that *the unconscious is unconscious,* always, which means that we cannot and do not experience it directly. The archetypes exist in the collective *un*conscious, so we cannot experience them directly either. We experience them as symbols and images. They are embodied as gods and goddesses, divine child and wisdom figure, great father and great mother, to name a few forms. For the Wordsworth of the "Intimations" Ode, the early sense of pure loss ("Whither is fled the visionary gleam? / Where is it now, the glory and the dream?") is answered, two years later, by his intuitive realization of the existence of the archetypes, that there are "truths that wake, / To perish never." It is as if, in those two years, the archetype of the knowing parent, which he had projected on to the earth, or nature, become instead part of Wordsworth's intuitive equipment: That is, he withdraws the projection, and the archetype enters into his consciousness, as when Athena guides Telemachus until he can be on his own. True, the awe that always surrounds the archetype is no longer felt in nature and so there is a sharp sense of loss, but there is also a new inner state. What was once magically "out there" has become the conviction "that in our embers / Is something that doth live."

Now suppose that the poet had not been able to do this: Suppose, that is, that the awed child had not been given the care and attention that Wordsworth gave it in the first four stanzas of the Ode. Suppose instead that the child had just pined away and died. What would this be like?

As we have seen, in *Power in the Helping Professions,* Adolf Guggenbuhl-Craig (1979) deals with exactly this question as it impinges upon the lives of teachers. If you will accept my argument that we all have within ourselves a teaching adult and a to-be-taught eager child, his argument applies to all of us. He writes:

The teacher-student encounter runs parallel to an inner tension between the states of being a knowledgeable adult and an unknowing child. In every adult there is a child who constantly leads us on to new things. The adult's knowledge makes him rigid and inaccessible to innovation. The unknowing child's irrational experimentation, his naive openness, must be retained as a living potential in every adult if he is to remain emotionally alive. . . .

Among the general public, school teachers are often accused of being infantile and unrealistic. This is not completely untrue. If one has many dealings with teachers one is soon reluctantly forced to admit a certain childishness and infantilism in their behavior. There must, after all, be something in the state of childishness which fascinates the teacher or else how could he spend his entire working time among children? . . .

The archetype by which the good teacher is fascinated is that of the knowing adult–unknowing child. (104–6)

As we have seen, Guggenbuhl-Craig goes on to make the point that if the inner child dies, the death of that child in the teacher is painful, so painful that the teacher cannot but repress the whole history of the loss. And who has not known such teachers? They go through the motions, but there is no energy in them, no sense of anything new to teach, or to learn. They are not connected *through the child* to the pupils in front of them; they have lost contact with what drew them into teaching in the first place, which is, as Guggenbuhl-Craig says, the uneasy but fascinating tension inside them, caused by the unknowing child–knowing adult archetype.

This tension is congruent with the tension in the "Intimations" Ode between the numinous, magical child and the older man who looks back with a sense of loss. This means that the reading—and the teaching—of this poem presents a very special opportunity. Perhaps we can arrange things so that the archetypal child will join up with us, not because it is in the poem, but because it is in us (and, if we teach, in our students) as well. This would be bringing together the three imaginal spaces—poem, students, and ourself. Here is a method designed to bring us in touch with our inner child. I propose a journey inward, to be recorded in journal entries. This is the method of the Progoff (1975) *Intensive Journal*. The difficulty we face in this journey is that *the world is too much with us.* In the busyness of our lives, we are, as e.e. cummings put it, caught in "ropes of thing."

So the first step is to become peaceful. We settle comfortably with writing materials nearby. It is necessary above all to be still. Then, in the stillness, address this question: "Where am I, now, in my life?" An answer may shape itself as a sentence beginning, "Now is a time in my life when I . . .," or there may come an image: "Now I am a rock." The important thing is to be open to whatever comes. This done, the next step is to take an inner inventory of this now-time: What other *people* have been especially important? What of your body: health or illness or drugs or sexuality or diet or exercise? What social issues have engaged you? What experiences with the arts, music, dance, theater? Have there been memorable dreams? Accidents of circumstance? Experiences of the spirit? Let such questions form, and write responses as they come; do not reject or censor.

As you hear me describe this work you may also be imagining your own response to it. But you are not now in that quiet space I described; you are reading. You are thinking about your journey inward, perhaps, but thinking about going inward is not the same thing as going inward. Given true quiet space, what you will then write may well be surprising, unexpectedly elating or sad, or previously absolutely unknown to you.

The surprise, or the deep feelings, come because we are, almost all of us, quite out of touch with this sort of quiet reflection. People who regularly meditate or who do spiritual exercises are more in tune with this work and therefore with themselves. I have found that this work, done with my students in classes, feels remarkable. Progoff speaks of "going down into the well of ourselves," and that is exactly the feeling. We lose sight of each other, of the classroom, of school, of the buzzing outside world.

The "now" time in our lives may have begun a few months ago, or years ago, or a few days ago: There is simply no telling. But we must begin with it; we cannot reflect on our history until we have a ground, a place on which to stand in the present. Wordsworth "positions" himself this way in the first four stanzas of the "Intimations" Ode. His "now" time, as he describes it there, is complex: He feels both the bliss of the morning *and* a pervasive but undefined sense of loss. Having positioned ourselves in our own "now" time, we too are prepared to look back.

We look back by listing what Progoff calls our *steppingstones*. Again we sit in meditative silence. In the quiet, we feel our life's journey. We feel the inner history of our life. A steppingstone is a time or an event when we moved from one way of being in our life to another; it is a marker along the path of our journey. At first these tend to be somewhat factual: I was born, we moved to the farm, my sister was born, and so on. But after several experiences of doing them, say over months or a year, steppingstones tend to become more metaphoric. Progoff provides an example from one of his journal workshops: "I was born. I loved. I danced. I wept. I posed. I suffered. I was entranced. I was humiliated. I got lost. I am trying to find my way" (1975, 111).

Each steppingstone, whether literal or metaphoric, has a reason for being. "Steppingstone" is itself a metaphor: a stone rising out of the stream, a place to step, a place to look backward and forward before moving on. We have, with our list, an inner as well as an outer history.

The third and last exercise is to imagine ourselves back on an earlier steppingstone, and then to write a dialogue between the person we are now and the person we were then. It is at this point that we may feel that a child has joined us, is talking with us. And that child often is not the child we remember being, but is instead an altogether unexpected other person. These dialogues often reveal startling things to my students—and even to me, as often as I have done them. (I do the journal work with my students in class.) We have much to learn from the child we were, because she or he is in part the archetypal child in us still. Because this is so, we have now created a situation that can mirror in us the imaginal space in which Wordsworth's great Ode may have been begun, that is, the space in which the inner child is imaged as lost, abandoned, and needy.

The child who joins us in dialogue sees the world differently from the way we do now, and we can feel his difference from us. The opening four stanzas of the Ode state that its speaker has lost an earlier way of seeing. There is no expressed or implied dialogue in these earlier stanzas; there is only the speaker wistfully remembering. The child comes to life in the later part of the poem:

Because we are asked to "Behold the child among his new-born blisses," we look at the child as a separate person, as we imagined ourselves to be in an earlier steppingstone, and we can feel an implied dialogue between the man who feels the loss and the youth who saw the earth "apparelled in celestial light." If we listen, if we imagine the speaker, we can feel the presence of the man and the youth, and we can feel the wistfulness in the one and the exuberant joy in nature of the other. Imagine the later part of the poem not as a poem but as a dramatic *situation* in which these two real people live and converse. When I see a psychotherapy patient in my office there are only the two of us there, and yet I find myself in a room filled with people. Between us we populate the room with children and parents and grandparents and teachers and lovers and shadowy figures of policemen and shining angels and people wearing masks and who knows who else. Places, too: the house of childhood, the rocks, the shoreline, a special tree. All of these come and go, encountering one another, talking and arguing in deep conversation, or splitting apart from one another, or making love or comforting a child or walking away just when the child is most lonely. It is not just therapy that creates this world. This is the world in which we all live, an imaginally created drama that is ours alone. So, too, we bring our inner drama to this poem, and because we do we can search for the imaginal space common to both us and the Ode.

I have suggested that the earlier part of the poem is a description of the gradual loss, in the poet, of his connection to the child archetype—the child who identifies itself with the divine in nature. It is no wonder that the ephemeral rainbow and rose are contrasted with the more permanent moon, water, and sun. The basic issue for any child is, can the world be trusted? The children gather flowers from the earth, which, motherlike, provides, and there is the child on its mother's arm—but all this is transitory, and therefore frightening. With the beginning of the later part of the poem, though, we have a denial that birth is unique for us. As "a sleep and a forgetting," birth is the moment when we are separated from the eternal realm of the archetypes; it is the moment when we become both human and individual at once and so lose sight of the soul, through which we were connected to the realm of the gods, the archetypes.

The child, though, does not feel this disconnection: It lives in the illusion that it is Godlike. A baby plays with a toy and then puts it down. We cover the toy with a corner of blanket and the baby looks elsewhere; the toy has ceased to exist because the baby can no longer see it. Seeing, for the baby, is creating: The baby is like the God of Genesis. This is true magic. Only gradually does the child learn that he is not God, not magic: "shades of the prison-house begin to close / Upon the growing boy." And indeed it is important not to stay overly close to the archetypes: that way lies pride, the deadliest of sins. "Inflation," Jung called it, a word denoting puffed up with air, or spirit: King Lear at the play's opening, confusing himself with Olympian Zeus. Earth, Wordsworth states, as our nurse, "doth all she can / To make her foster-child, her inmate man, / Forget the glories he hath known, / And that imperial palace whence he came" (lines 81–84). Earth, as the mother archetype, knows what's what, and grounds us—literally.

But disconnection from the archetypes brings with it loss, and so alienation: "Full soon thy soul shall have her earthly freight, / And custom lie upon thee with a weight, / Heavy as frost, and deep almost as life!" Is this inevitable? Is aging only and always loss? The poet finds a new way, in the time of life which I take as adolescence. Of delight and liberty, the simple creed of childhood, he says he is not thankful. Rather, he is thankful for

> those obstinate questionings
> Of sense and outward things,
> Fallings from us, vanishings,
> Blank misgivings of a creature
> Moving about in worlds not realized. (lines 141–45)

Is there a better description of adolescence than this? Have any of us not heard and felt our obstinate questionings, our vanishings, our blank misgivings, and, above all, our yearning toward a world not realized? And did we not feel these things in ourselves?

And so we grow, as the years pass; and with time we reach that point in our lives when the archetypes reappear, not as our whole world, not as our entire being, but as

> moments in the being
> Of the eternal silence—truths that wake,
>   To perish never,
> Which neither listlessness nor mad endeavor,
>   Nor man nor boy,
> Nor all that is at enmity with joy,
> Can utterly abolish or destroy!
>   Hence in a season of calm weather,
>   Though inland far we be,
> Our souls have sight of that immortal sea
>   Which brought us hither,
>   Can in a moment travel thither,
> And see the children sport upon the shore,
> And hear the mighty waters rolling evermore. (lines 154–67)

So the pattern of this great, courageous poem is to be seen as a going out and a returning, as the child going forth, but slowly finding that it is human and thus unable to remain in the realm of heroes and gods; then, relinquishing them as he must, as he grows, he returns with the wisdom that follows loss. His wisdom is that he can at last contain in a single vision the children and the great ocean, the numinous child and the source of all life seen together. This the soul sees. For the child *is* father of the man, if the child is seen as archetype, as source of energy and connectedness and renewal, all needed for our life's journey. Wordsworth knew always that he must keep the child within him to remain whole. But he came to see that the ocean must be there too—the opposites of ephemeral child and eternal waters must be held together in the imagination as they are in dreams. When they are so held, we can feel, with the poet at Tintern Abbey,

> that serene and blessed mood
> In which the affections gently lead us on,
> Until, the breath of this corporeal frame
> And even the motion of our human blood
> Almost suspended, we are laid asleep
> In body and become a living soul,
> While, with an eye made quiet by the power
> Of harmony and the deep power of joy,
> We see into the life of things. ("Tintern Abbey," lines 41–48)

Such a vision of seeing into the life of things is the vision of the archetypal wisdom figure, the counterpart of the child. The return to Tintern Abbey was the occasion for an experience of the wisdom figure, of which Prospero is the supreme emblem in literature, and whose words so resemble Wordsworth's: Just as Wordsworth says we reach a state where we are "laid asleep / In body and become a living soul," so Prospero says,

> We are such stuff
> As dreams are made on, and our little life
> Is rounded with a sleep.
> —*The Tempest*, Act 4, Scene 1

But this is the vision of wisdom, the vision near the end, and it is a vision brought on by sleep, by the loss of consciousness; it is Wordsworth's somewhat abstract sense of what the world of archetypes would be like. It is wonderful, but the tension is muted, minimal.

By contrast, in the "Intimations" Ode, Wordsworth faces the wonder and the fear and the tension of child and wisdom figure facing each other across the years. In the Ode, as in us, things are not yet worked out; there is pain and loss *and* joy and wisdom. Through this poem we feel the child in us, and the journey of our own lives as well:

> Though nothing can bring back the hour
> Of splendour in the grass, of glory in the flower,
>     We will grieve not, rather find
>     Strength in what remains behind. (lines 177–80)

Wisdom and pain of loss go together, each informing and nurturing the other. In this poem we have not the sense of resolution represented by Prospero but the struggle toward that resolution, a struggle that makes us vulnerable because to be aware of it we must be open to ourselves.

Wordsworth, at the end of the poem, gives thanks for his openness to the shared ground of feelings:

> Thanks to the human heart by which we live———
> Thanks to its tenderness, its joys, and fears———
> To me the meanest flower that blows can give
> Thoughts that do often lie too deep for tears. (lines 199–202)

We, too, when we touch the archetypes, have such thoughts. Deep as they are, they are the fountainhead of all our days. At this point we have approached the ground of being that makes it possible for us, as teachers, to work in the imaginal space we share with both writer and student. It is a place where there is no longer any distinction between teacher and taught, between reader and writer. The operative, crucial word is *shared*. The story, when all goes well, creates a shared space. And that, in the end, is what art is for.

## NOTE

1. Schwartz's resonance principle is congruent with Vygotsky's concept of the Zone of Proximal Space: "the distance between the actual developmental level as determined by independent problem solving and the level of potential development as determined through problem solving under adult guidance or in a collaboration with more capable peers." In other words, when the student, because of the presence of the teacher, does something he didn't know he could do, it is because the teacher has created a space congruent with a construct latent in the student but unavailable to him. See Bruner 1986, 70–78, from which the quote above is taken. My own view is that students first project such knowledge on to the teacher and then, as their competence develops, withdraw the projection. But if the reward of controlling (by frustrating) the teacher is greater than the reward of the new competence, students will persist in not understanding.

## WORKS CITED

Bruner, Jerome. *Actual Minds, Possible Worlds*. Cambridge, Massachusetts: Harvard University Press, 1986.

Guggenbuhl-Craig, Adolf. *Power in the Helping Professions*. Dallas: Spring Publications, 1979.

Jung, C. G. *Symbols of Transformation*. Vol. 5 of *The Collected Works of C. G. Jung*. 20 vols. Princeton, New Jersey: Bollingen Series XX, Princeton University Press, 1956.

———. *Freud and Psychoanalysis*. Vol. 4 of *The Collected Works of C. G. Jung*. 20 vols. Princeton, New Jersey: Bollingen Series XX, Princeton University Press, 1970.

Progoff, Ira. *At a Journal Workshop*. New York: Dialogue House Library, 1975.

Rosowski, Susan J. *The Voyage Perilous*. Lincoln: University of Nebraska Press, 1986.

Schwartz, Tony. *The Responsive Chord*. New York: Doubleday, Anchor Press, 1974.

Shakespeare, William. *The Tempest*. Ed. Northrop Frye. Baltimore: Penguin Books, 1959.

Wordsworth, William. *William Wordsworth: An Illustrated Selection*. Ed. Jonathan Wordsworth. Grasmere, Cumbria: The Wordsworth Trust, 1987.

## Chapter Five

# When Nothing Works: Despair, Alienation, and Shadow

*Prospero*: This thing of darkness
I acknowledge mine.

—*The Tempest*, Act 5, Scene 1

Ms. Shepley's first class that morning at Lakeview High School was an easy one for her to teach partly because it had so few students in it. As the day went on, though, other, more well-attended classes followed, and they brought problems. Students whispered to each other, or passed notes, or tried to sleep. But Ms. Shepley's informal and affable demeanor did good service for her; she was able to defuse potential problems gently. She was never caught, as I had been that day so many years before in the Natick High School lunch room, by a need to prove her authority, her power. Nevertheless she, and almost every other beginning teacher I've seen, was never truly at ease. In the back of her mind, she told me—when I asked her—she had the feeling that something, something bad, was always about to happen. And this was so even though things were going well. Furthermore, she knew that some of her student-teaching colleagues were having real trouble. In the University of Illinois program, all the student teachers in English come to the campus each Wednesday afternoon for a seminar. It is a seminar in name only. What really happens is a sharing of things that worked and things that didn't, together with suggestions from me, and from the other supervisors. Frustration and feelings of helplessness are part of the picture, especially at the beginning of each term. These feelings are natural enough, to be sure, but beginning teachers are never well prepared for them. Overwhelmingly the feelings derive from a simple fact. It is that the students in the schools—the eighth graders, the eleventh graders, the bright and the slow—are not what *our* students expected them to be. Our students enjoyed school and were pretty good at it (Why else would they want to teach?), but *their* students are sullen, resentful, and argumentative. They don't seem to be interested in *anything* the English curriculum has to offer. Their lives are elsewhere, and, in the city, the elsewhere is often frighteningly other: drugs, abuse, gangs, unwanted pregnancy, chaos at home.

We know who they are and we know what they do to us, the alienated ones, those students so far removed from our values, our beliefs, our whole way of life. An experienced teacher wrote to the editor of the *English Journal* (1989) of her despair. The very beginning of the letter speaks of the feeling, shared by many teachers, of "*utter and total helplessness.*" No feeling could be worse when it comes from our chosen work, and is caused by the very people we have chosen to work with. At the same time we know there are some teachers who succeed, against all odds, with these very students. This hurts even more, because it suggests that only a few gifted teachers, ourselves not included, can do this work. Students in teacher education programs often feel this way at the beginning of their practice teaching. Is this really so? Or are there certain things we can all do?

There are, I believe, things to be done, and I will list some of them shortly. But the larger and more pervasive problem is the "otherness" of students. I have mentioned this in connection with typology. But the problem is deeper than that. These difficult students are not only difficult in themselves. They are the outcasts of society, the underclass. They are everything, it seems, that we are not. No wonder they are so hard to reach.

But they also represent a deeply buried part of ourselves: our *shadow*. Pogo's famous observation is apt: we have met the enemy and they are us. It is not easy to accept the idea that we have in ourselves a rebellious, angry part. For this reason I will take up the issue of shadow last. In order to lead up to the problem gently, I begin with the more practical, "outer" aspects of working with difficult students.

Here are three suggestions, three tasks to carry out. Doing each one successfully enables us to say to ourselves, and anyone else, that we have done all we can do as classroom teachers. Saying that is what keeps despair at bay. What are the three tasks? Simply put, they are:

1. To distinguish between the possible and the impossible; that is, to separate problems where our work in the classroom can make a difference from problems over which we have no control;

2. To find curriculum content that is interesting and involving to *us*, because only then will it be involving for these students; and,

3. To face and come to acknowledge, in ourselves, some of the very feelings and behaviors we find so appalling in our most difficult students. What we represent to these students is as strange and upsetting as what they represent to us: The common ground we share with them is the very alienation that seems to be their basic problem. These students are our shadow, as we are theirs. We must learn to recognize, and then use, this difficult kinship.

Let us look at these three tasks.

## THE POSSIBLE AND THE IMPOSSIBLE

Some years ago, I asked my English Department colleagues in an inner-city high school to list two problems they felt they faced in their work. Here are some of their items. Try to decide which are addressable in the classroom and which are not:

— Poor background—foundations of students very poor.

— Teachers in other areas of instruction unconcerned.

— Students who have not been taught the basic mechanics before ninth grade.

— Class time does not afford enough time for coverage of some lessons.

— To get students to have an open mind to accept new material.

— Not having enough textbooks for my classes. I have one set for five classes.

— Motivation—trying to impart some idea of the value to each pupil in terms of his own life as to how what is being done can serve him.

— My greatest problem is teaching . . . what I am not prepared to teach. As an English major, I was not prepared to teach remedial reading or basic grammar.

Let us look at these.

First, *poor background.* Phrased this way, it seems unaddressable; what can a teacher do about what's happened in the past? But try this translation: "These students have a background that differs from mine." Suddenly the problem becomes at least partly addressable by means of comparison/contrast. Students are fascinated by their teachers' lives. Use that. This means, for example, doing exercises from *At a Journal Workshop* (Progoff 1975) in which teacher and students together explore where they are now in their lives and how they got to where they are. (For example, in the "Period Log" exercise, we begin by writing, together with our students, in a serious and quiet atmosphere, an answer to the question, "Where am I now, in my life?" The question itself is so unusual, and so immediate, that the treasured silence follows it, in my experience. And the writing may stay private; it need not be handed in. It is the beginning of journal-keeping, parts of which will eventually be shared. The idea of teachers writing with their students is of course a staple of the Writing Projects, and is, I feel, essential with alienated students.) But beyond this one bit of technique, background is an unaddressable problem. We cannot undo and re-form the pasts of our students. Our work is in the present. A classroom with difficult students in it is like the emergency room in a city hospital. Our task is to treat the presenting problem *now*, as fast and as accurately as we can. A fourteen-year-old girl whose kneecap has been shattered by a stray bullet fired in a drug war needs to be treated for shock, stabilized, and taken to surgery. It proves nothing to consider the state of her neighborhood, the drug problem locally or nationally, or even what she was doing on the street at 2 A.M.

Similarly, and especially with alienated students, the only time that matters is right now. The world happens in now time, from these students' point of view, and it is essential for us to recognize this and act upon it. The past is done and the future is mostly unimaginable. (The typology of extraverted sensation does have something to do with this.)

Second, *other areas of instruction* (I think this means other teachers) unconcerned. Unaddressable. Our domain is our own classroom. What other teachers do or don't do can only be addressed if one of those other people asks us something. Otherwise, it's not up to us to take it on. Setting the tone or mood of a school is what administrators get paid (a lot) to do. When they succeed we benefit. When they fail, the privacy of our classroom is our refuge. Besides, energy spent blaming others is mostly wasted, and energy is a precious commodity. One day (in the cafeteria of this same school) we were having yet another gripe session when a colleague suddenly got up to leave. "I can't sit in on this any more; it eats my liver," she said. She was right, and wise.

*No basic mechanics taught earlier.* This is a variant of the background issue, and it has the same partial cure: *Use* our difference, and be careful not to scapegoat either the students or their former teachers. Most of us who teach English know basic mechanics not because we were taught them or learned them, but because we grew up in homes where they were already in place. That's our difference. It can be talked about. Conventional language patterns are also used on most television shows. Use them; get students to listen to how Bill Cosby or Bob Newhart speak. Blaming parents and earlier teachers is futile, and will eat our livers.

*Not enough time.* Obviously addressable: Do less. But why is it listed by this teacher, when the solution is so obvious? Because it's an excuse: It says, in effect, "I could do more, but *they*—the bell-ringers and schedule-makers—won't let me." The overall school schedule is not addressable. It's in the domain of the administration, where it belongs. Scapegoating them will also eat our livers. Of course it's always possible to *try* to work with administrators. But in general, our task as teachers is to make do with what we have. This is a variant of the more general problem posed by the teacher who wrote to the *English Journal*: "There is little individual teachers can do (often nothing!) in the situation." Such a view leads on to feelings of helplessness.

*Getting students to have an open mind.* Addressable if *we* have such a mind, especially a mind open to anger and frustration and what they make us do. See below, about our own shadow, and self-knowledge.

*Not enough textbooks.* Addressable: think of it as a blessing. It probably is.

*Motivation*—how what is being done [in class] can be useful, can serve the pupil. This is addressable, but only if we stop thinking about what students "should" know and start looking at what they do know. Students, especially the most difficult ones, have stringent tests of what's useful, and they apply them constantly. That's one reason why writing from out of their own lives, but in an organized and sympathetic way, as in the journal work, can be effective. Another approach here is to teach something so outlandishly useless that we get mock open rebellion, not real rebellion. This is the "judo" theory of motivation. It fits with the idea that what matters is what's happening now. The fact that you think literacy will be useful some day for your students is as irrelevant as it is obvious.

*As an English major, I'm not prepared to teach these people.* Addressable. This teacher should go watch the teachers who are good at it, and imitate what they do: shop teachers, coaches, anybody who gets good work out of the students. That's how to really learn. Nobody fresh out of a teacher education program, or any other kind of school, is prepared for anything. Medical school graduates—first year residents—are almost useless as doctors; the smart ones learn from the nurses. They aren't prepared to start an IV drip or explain a procedure (their equivalents of remedial reading and basic grammar) either. More subtly, the English major this teacher had in college probably created a huge gap between him or her and students who live so far away from the best that has been thought and written. English can be a pretty fancy study. Again: Our work is in the emergency room, not in the rare book library.

Most problems, in short, are addressable; if not concretely, then by adopting a different stance, or point of view, or way of looking at the situation. But some problems are not addressable. These we must ignore if we are to succeed.

## CURRICULUM—FOR OURSELVES

It is fatal to try to succeed with materials of little or no interest to us. The reason for this is that true learning happens only in those classrooms where the students feel that the teacher is learning too. Good teaching, I say again, is not done to students; it is done with them. "With" means just that: learning together. If they feel we know and they don't, then we have all the power available in the classroom. That creates a feeling which is anathema to difficult students. Their lives are full of people who try to have power over them: parents, bosses, lovers, false friends, police. Seldom—very seldom—has any adult ever said to them, "Let's work on this together and see what's going on," or, "I don't get this. Help me out." These are wonderful ways to begin discussion, and they are wonderful things to write on student papers, *but we have to really mean them.* There are many situations where we can really want students' help: Ann Landers's column is full of them. Asking them what they would do about the problems she deals with honors the fact that they have lived in the world and had experience in it and of it. And honoring these students will make us feel better about ourselves—part of the cure for despair, surely.

Another part of doing things for ourselves is to choose curriculum materials of interest solely to us and then use our enthusiasm as the bridge to our students. I remember some years ago doing a unit on the history of the English language in that inner-city school. One assignment was to memorize The Lord's Prayer in Old English: "Faeder ure, [th]u [th]e eart on heofonum, Tobecume [th]in rice . . ." The weirdness of it made it an enormous hit. My students were sure they were the only people anywhere in Chicago who knew this stuff (they were probably right) and they derived a lot of pride from being different. They were different because they knew the Old English, and I was different because they'd never known anyone else crazy enough to be interested in Old English in the first place. (They could see my child's excitement there, too.) We all felt good. This is an example of what I meant by the "judo" theory of motivation: using our energy to tap energy that's already in the students, rather than just putting all our own energy to work against theirs, a sure pathway to exhaustion. Besides, the history of the language explains language difference, and so it gave us a way to study dialect, a most relevant and useful topic in a school whose enrollment was almost entirely Black.

I could have learned to follow my own enthusiasms a lot earlier in my teaching career, but I didn't, for reasons that I think matter here. In my first year of teaching, as I've said, I asked my most difficult class—the "general" track—to write what they felt about our brand-new high school building, of which the administration, the teachers, and the citizens were all very proud. The students hated it, it turned out; they much preferred the old, run-down building they'd just left. You may recall that in the old building they could hide out in the basement, sneak around in the corridors, and generally be on their own. The new building was all glassed-in corridors and an enclosed "campus"—nowhere to hide. The old building let them have a secret life the school officially denied them. We wrote and discussed this until the students became anxious and wanted to get back to "English." And "English," for them, didn't work. I now know that nothing works if it consists only of what "should" be taught—whether the "should" comes from the curriculum, the administration, the citizens, or even the students themselves. (James Herndon's perfect title, *The Way It Spozed To Be* (Herndon 1969) captures the whole problem, but I started teaching long before that splendid book was written.) When the students asked for "English," I got pressured from the establishment already so well established within me, instead of recognizing that the wonderful writing they were doing *was* English. The result was that we returned to noisy classes and sullen resentment on both sides; those bad habits that are so discouraging but which are, alas, "the way it spozed to be." I was also afraid someone was watching: department head or principal. No one was, of course. The classroom is a fine and private place indeed, but I had all the paranoia of the beginning teacher. It took me several years to realize that, as a teaching tool, the door is as important as the blackboard. I should have stayed within the privileged, private world I had stumbled into.

The curriculum has to be what *we* care about. And as I've said about story, curriculum comes from our shared experience of the journey of our lives. "Shared" is the key. If it is not shared it will fail. Nothing done solely for the good of "them," or because we "should" do it, will work.

## OUR SHADOW, OURSELVES

Alienated students, many of them, lead lives that are unimaginable to us: violence, drugs, physical and sexual abuse, children having children—we know the litany. And lesser horrors: too many people living in too little space, never enough money unless drugs or prostitution become part of the life, and so on. We grit our teeth in the morning to keep this world out, and we flee it in the afternoon, grateful if our car has not been broken into. How can this dreadful world possibly be a part of us? But it is, even though it is a world of anger, frustration, resentment, loss, and deprivation.

Think about those words. Are we not also angry and frustrated and resentful? Clearly the writer to the *English Journal* felt these things. But what do we do with these feelings? "Nicely" brought up as we are, we don't display them, especially in front of students. They, on the other hand, do display them, and our resentment increases—not only because they're being rude and difficult, *but also because they are showing, out in the world, exactly what we are feeling, privately and inside.*

What we share with these students, with all students, with everyone, is *shadow*. *Shadow* is a term of Jung's, the word he used to denote "all that which we would least want to be." For Jung shadow is a natural and inevitable component in everyone's psyche. (Jung said that even God cannot be complete without a shadow. In "Answer to Job" [Jung 1969] Jung used as an example the fact that God enters into a bet with the devil over Job, surely a perverse thing to do. And it is the shadow side of God that orders Abraham to kill Isaac. God's shadow, Jung wrote, is the part of God that *needs human attention*. For that matter, Job has a shadow too—his own "virtue." Jung wrote, "If Job succeeds in [coming to know] his shadow he will be deeply ashamed. . . . He will see that he has only to accuse himself, for it is his complacency, his righteousness, his literal-mindedness, etc., which have brought all evil down upon him.") In this connection too it is useful to remember Prospero's explanation of the monster, Caliban, to the ship-wrecked nobility at the end of the play: "This thing of darkness I acknowledge mine." Another example is the relationship between Peter Pan and Captain Hook. For Peter adulthood is, of course, to be resisted at all costs: Adulthood is a big part of Peter's shadow. But for Hook, the impulsive and fun-loving child, Peter, is an emblem of *his* shadow. Each therefore hates the other.

Ask yourself what sort of person would you least like to be, or least like to meet up with on a dark night in a strange neighborhood, and you may well get an image of what a part of your shadow is like. Such figures in dreams often illustrate aspects of the dreamer's shadow. Unknown and threatening as they are, they are part of us. After all, we create our own dreams.

How does our shadow turn up in the teaching of English? One way is in our willful teaching of useless and, yes, even perverse material. Not us, you say? Consider: Even though the research overwhelmingly demonstrates that the teaching of traditional grammar has no effect, or even a negative effect, on writing or speaking skills, it is nevertheless taught ubiquitously, and especially to the students of lowest ability. This teaching often proceeds thus: Teacher: "A verb is a word that shows action or state of being." Student: "You mean, like *explosion*? That's got action." Teacher: "No, Lemuel, explosion's a noun, don't you see? Remember? A noun is the name of a person, a place or thing." A brash student would ask, "If explosion's a thing, how come I can't bring you one?" But brashness never pays off, a lesson Lemuel has learned all too well, and so sullen incomprehension is the result of this little exchange. How long before this turns to anger only Lemuel knows. But turn it will.

This insistence on the irrational and the incomprehensible is carried over into the inane questions in literature anthologies and the exercises in the grammar handbooks. (The teacher's handbook for a British Literature anthology had this item in one of its suggested tests: "Hamlet is a ———— .") Why, in the face of so much enlightened criticism of them, do such inane activities and questions persist?

Ignorance alone can't explain it. The fact is that these perverse activities express a part of our shadow: our need to have power over the students who most scare us, who most threaten us. They scare us because they represent our own impulsiveness, our own destructiveness, perhaps especially our own anger and prejudice. Shadow—our own shadow—is ugly. Our need for power is especially ugly, even though it is a need germinated in the soil of our helplessness. But face this we must, if we are to reach these alienated students. Our own anger, however expressed, has to be understood and appreciated by us for what it is: anger at *them*, and anger at our own helplessness as well. So our shadow side says, in effect, *since they make me feel helpless, I'll make them feel helpless too, by asking them to do incomprehensible and useless activities.* Only when we put this card face up can we see it.

It's not anger itself that's bad. There's good anger, as when we rip a student for doing a poor job when we know the student has just goofed off. This is the good anger of the coach who benches a player during the big game because of lack of hustle. Good anger shows the student that we care *and* that we believe the student is capable of good work. Bad anger is concealed; it lurks in the illogical definitions, the cart-before-the-horse curricula that substitute scanning poetry for understanding it, that foist fill-in-the-blanks worksheets on students in place of real writing. The curriculum is the easiest place to find, and weed out, instances of our exercise of covert power over our students. But we must also look very closely at those little exchanges like the one about "explosion." Every day of teaching we have hundreds of such little conversations. We need to be sure they make sense, that they are honest, rather than covert expressions of our need to be in control. Not outward control in the sense of classroom management—that's obviously necessary and desirable—but, rather, the insidious control that comes from keeping what we teach just slightly incomprehensible, and thus keeping it to ourselves.

Education in general, and teacher education in particular, is still dominated by an eighteenth-century ideal: that reason ultimately defeats whatever stands in its way. Truth is equated with logic. And "reason" is understood as the property of the dominant culture. Any other self-sustaining culture is likely to be felt as shadow. Efforts to redress this problem, by including Black, Native American or Hispanic Studies—and Women's Studies—in a school or university may do some good, but the question remains whether such work addresses the deeper level contained in shadow. Any such programs could well remain one-sided, by merely imposing the same eighteenth-century rationality on their particular subject matters. This one-sidedness has devastating consequences. It encourages students throughout their whole education to emphasize ego (hard work will be rewarded, and enable you to be the "hero" of your own life) and persona (learn what you need to know and do, in order to "fit in"). The dark side of the inner worlds of teacher and student is simply ignored in most educational enterprises. Consequently the personal and the idiosyncratic become part of the shadow of our educational institutions. For shadow has two origins and two settings: personal and collective.

Our personal shadow forms whenever we are told, as children, what not to do, whom to avoid, what to fear. More subtly, it forms when we intuit that there are things we are *not* being told; things feared by the adults around us. This avoidance, and the fear behind it, are sensed by children. Here is an example of my own.

When I was very small my parents and I lived on a chicken farm in what was then rural New Jersey. One day we had a delivery of coal: The coal was simply dumped into the basement from a truck that pulled up beside our house. I had never seen this procedure before and I was fascinated. And I had never seen people such as the ones delivering the coal: They were black. (This was in 1938, well before TV, and well before black people were pictured in advertisements in the newspapers or magazines around our house.) As soon as I could I found a woman I knew— she worked for us—and asked her about these strange-looking men. I imagine she was troubled by my question: How to explain this part of *her* shadow to a small boy? In any case, this is what she told me. She said that the men were black because they worked with coal every day. Of course I soon learned the truth, but the rational truth has little effect on the unconscious development of shadow: There was something about black people she could not acknowledge, something that prevented her from telling me the truth. And her avoidance—or, rather, the feeling behind her avoidance—stayed with me. It still does, tempered, I hope, by some gain in experience and understanding. But this is how shadow, personal shadow, develops: from these exchanges about, and experiences of, what is unknown and threatening to others and to ourselves, that we have as we grow up.

The collective shadow is an extension of this: It is those things that our group, our race, our social peers, our fellow tennis club members, our bridge club, our bowling team—repudiate, shun, make fun of, or fear. Insofar as we go along to get along, we will adopt these attitudes. Schools are redolent with the collective shadow, both in the hallways and in the teacher's cafeteria.

So shadow is there, personally and in the collective. It is the dark side. In teaching it comes out, as I have said, in punitive and irrational curricula, in the teaching of materials which are left unexplained. Under the idea of "learn this because it's good for you" there is surely anger. Where poetry is taught by emphasizing scansion, metric patterns, and tropes—iambs, trochees, metonymy—instead of meaning and value; where description is substituted for imaginal entering of the work: here anger lurks. Such teaching reserves poetry for the teacher. And that is an angry thing to do.

Facing our own anger and seeing how it may emerge subtly in class is one example of recognizing our shadow side. Essentially our problem is a moral one, not a curricular one. Any set of materials, any curriculum—yes, even traditional grammar, if taught by a person passionately, truthfully convinced that it is important, and matters, for teacher and students—will work. But anything taught insincerely, or out of an even unconscious need for power, is doomed. When our students come to sense that we are trying to deal with these things ourselves, and therefore trying to be *equal with them* in our concern for what matters, our connection with them will deepen, and the climate in the classroom will change for the better. This is a deep and difficult road, this facing our own shadow. The need for power runs deep in teaching and schooling. But if we can honestly say we have tried to face the shadow in ourselves, and found what *we* want to teach, and sorted out the possible from the impossible, then we have done as much as can be expected of us. Our most difficult students will then know we have done all that we can. We can ask no more of ourselves, and neither can they. If things still fail—and obviously they sometimes will—we can at least know we have reached the limit of what we can do. We can then say, together with Samuel Beckett's tramps, waiting for Godot, that "we have kept our appointment," our appointment with the ideals that brought us to this excruciatingly difficult work in the first place. Reconnecting with those ideals will defend us against despair. Knowing that our most difficult students mirror the dark part of ourselves will help us build bridges to them. But of all the work of teaching, this is surely the most difficult.

## WORKS CITED

*English Journal.* "Editorial Comments," 78, No. 6, October 1989, 56.

Herndon, James. *The Way It Spozed To Be.* New York: Bantam Books, 1969.

Jung, C. G. "Answer to Job." *Psychology and Religion: East and West.* Vol. 11 of *The Collected Works of C. G. Jung.* 20 vols. Princeton, New Jersey: Bollingen Series XX, Princeton University Press, 1969.

Progoff, Ira. *At a Journal Workshop.* New York: Dialogue House Library, 1975.

## Chapter Six

# Teaching at the Edge: Dressing the Unknowable in the Garments of the Known

*Prospero*:  (Aside) The charm dissolves apace,
And as the morning steals upon the night,
Melting the darkness, so their rising senses
Begin to chase the ignorant fumes that mantle
Their clearer reason.—

—*The Tempest*, Act 5, Scene 1

We have looked at the craft of teaching and how that craft is learned, and we have explored relationship as it develops in the classroom. And we have looked at power and shadow, the dark side of teaching. The intricacy and the difficulty of the work are, I hope, clear. Nevertheless we know that there are many teachers who not only stay with the work for a lifetime but who are nourished and enlivened by it. This chapter is about why this can be so. It returns to Robert Carlsen's three stages of a teacher's life: survival, mastering the given curriculum, and then (in my view of it) connecting one's teaching, through the energy of the child, to one's own life's journey. Teaching in the third stage is represented by Hermes, the god of threshold-crossing and message-bringing. That is what this chapter is about. Teaching in a fourth stage (the subject of my final chapter) is represented by Shakespeare's

Prospero, who in the end abjures, as he says, the "rough magic" he has practiced. This chapter is a description of that point at which teaching intersects with those timeless forms, the archetypes, in particular with Hermes, the messenger of the gods.

On its face this seems to be an exalted, even inflated claim. Teaching, especially school teaching, is a work for which the rest of the public has little respect. And teaching is a "flat" career. There are no rewards to be had from increased responsibility. True, one's salary does go up year by year, but there is no connection between the salary and the quality of the teaching being done. Good teachers and bad ones make the same money and earn the same increases. People who work in "the real world" have little respect for such a system.

There may have been a time when a school teacher was a respected, even honored, member of the community, but not, it seems to me, within living memory. Part of the problem is that no one, save teachers themselves, know how difficult and demanding the work can be. The reason for this is that teaching is done in private, in the sense that seldom, if ever, does another adult enter a classroom and watch teaching going on. And so, year in and year out, the work goes on, but without the approbation and the camaraderie that most work settings provide. In this loneliness teachers grow, not only, one hopes, through Carlsen's three stages, but also into the conviction that their work matters. Alas, such a conviction is by no means universally forthcoming. As I've said, half of the young people who start out in teaching have left the classroom after five years. Many others who stay on either never get to Carlsen's fulfilling third stage or, if they do, their energy is so drained by the work demanded that they retreat, with accompanying guilt, to the second stage, as I indicated earlier.

In his book *Ministry Burnout* Sanford (1982, 5–16) provides a list of the "special difficulties" ministering people face in their work. Because so many of these difficulties apply to teaching as well, I want to list several of them. As you read them, gauge for yourself whether you've felt them in your own life. I've substituted "teaching" for his "ministering" throughout.

*The job of a teacher is never finished.* There is no time, not even on the last day of school in June, when a teacher can really say, "There, I'm finished." Teaching is not like cooking a meal or building a table or painting a room. To be sure, the school year ends in June, but that's an ending, not a finishing. There's a big difference. How can we ever say that a class is "finished" with *Hamlet*? Or with ideas about how language works? Or with anything that we, as English teachers, teach?

*Teachers cannot tell if their work is having any results.* For English teaching to make any difference, the results have to be inside our students. Testing such inner happenings is subtle and difficult. Perhaps the most rewarding "good results" are to be found in wonderful student writing, but how can we know whether what we did made that happen? Cause and effect in teaching is subtle at best. As Janet Emig (1983, 135) puts it, we know that teachers teach and that children learn, but we cannot prove that children learn *because* teachers teach. To assume cause and effect is to invoke magic. Decades of research on teacher effectiveness have given us no consensus about what good teaching might be. Art and science, skill and luck; we know we need all of these, but we still can't necessarily see that we're having an effect. Adolescents are masters at masking what they really feel about what we do. It just isn't cool to be interested in class. Their lack of interest, whether it is real or a pose, undermines us to the point where the question "Am I making any difference?" can become a haunting, perhaps even debilitating concern—especially if we have honestly faced the presence of our own shadow in the classroom.

*The work of the teacher is repetitive.* In the first few years of a teaching career, this isn't much of a problem. But how many times can we take tenth graders through "Stopping by Woods on a Snowy Evening"? How long does it take before we know in advance what questions they will have? How long does it take before the poem ceases to work in *us*, sounding, instead, like a name repeated over and over again until it has no meaning?

*Teachers deal constantly with people's expectations.* Our own students, their parents, the administration, the school board, the citizens who (reluctantly, passively, or even angrily) pay our salary; all of these have expectations of us. But will these people help us with our work? Probably not. Even though we need their help, we instead hear only about what they want.

*The teacher must work with the same people year in and year out.* When I first read this in Sanford's list, I saw that it applied to ministers in a parish, but I thought it was one problem we teachers escape. Our students, after all, do change every year, or even every semester. But in a larger sense, students are students. The way adolescents are doesn't change very much, year in and year out: Their customs change, to be sure, but the basic elements of adolescence—the confusion about identity, the restless searching, the laziness, the lack of focus or the over-focus on one thing (a car, say, or good looks) to the exclusion of all else—such is the adolescent, year after year. And, because so few new teachers are entering the system (although there are more coming in now), most of us have tended to work with the same group of adults, our colleagues, year in and year out as well. So the natural stimulus of newness is not very available to us.

*Because we work with people in need, there is a particularly great drain on the energy of teachers.* This means that we are always giving something of ourselves. To stay in equilibrium, a system needs to get back what it gives: In a good marriage, for example, the partners give and get from each other pretty equally. If this ceases to be so, the marriage is in trouble. But in teaching, do we get back more than we give? I can't answer that question generally, but every teacher can find his or her particular answer, and feel its consequences. Another related question is to ask ourselves how much, at this time in our lives, we feel we have available to give to our students. When we feel a lessening of the energy and enthusiasm we can still bring to our teaching, we are measuring how we are against our memories of how we were.

*Teachers must function a great deal of time on* persona. The *persona* is the "front," or mask, or image that we create for ourselves to meet up with the world around us, and especially with the people in that world. A persona is necessary. It makes clear to other people who we are, and it protects us from having to be completely open to other people every waking minute. When a persona is dropped, it usually isn't dropped for very long, and the results may be wonderful or awful or somewhere in between. "Boy, she really let her hair down in there!" is a reaction (complete with appropriate metaphor) to that person's having dropped her persona, and what was briefly seen was more genuine, but not necessarily more helpful or constructive. Such behavior might make a mess of a faculty meeting or cause problems with the principal. But it could be useful, too. It all depends on the particular situation.

The persona is an especially important part of a teacher's inner makeup. It is what our students see most of the time, and they can sense unerringly whether it is closely connected with, or far away from, the rest of our psyche. The greater the distance between our teaching persona and the rest of what we are, the greater the strain teaching will put on us.

*Teachers may become exhausted by failure.* This is related to the issue of whether we see any results; seeing no results would surely bring feelings of failure. But the failure I have in mind here is more pervasive. It goes to the question of whether what we believe and value, and therefore try to teach, really has any effect in the world at large. We see everywhere distortions of language, censorship of books and ideas, lives lived in the absence of books and ideas, lives lived in the absence of reflection, reading, or even thought; lives lived in rigidity, in fear of any sort of change, let alone growth. In short, does what we do matter in a world where getting a job—*any* job—is all that really counts? The world of get-it-while-you-can and the world of ideas are in dire and constant conflict. To the extent we feel discouraged about how that conflict is going, we can be haunted by a sense of failure: We cannot seem to make what matters to us matter to others, even though it is our work to try to do so.

I would venture that almost none of this is what we thought we would feel when we decided to make teaching our life's work. I want to trace, now, the journey many of us have traveled since we made the decision to become teachers.

For many of us who teach English, the beginning, the first inkling that teaching might be our life, came, as I've said, through a sense of the joy of reading. A story, a play, a poem transported us, gave us an alternative world of experience. For some of us the joy might have been in language itself: in its sounds and its effects. The operative word here is *joy*: pure, unalloyed fun. In some cases the fun was our own discovery; in other cases, the joy came through a teacher we were lucky enough to have at the right time in our lives. There is both a sense of complete involvement here, and something more: the willing suspension of disbelief, the freely given surrender of one's self to the world created in one's mind by the book. This is "play" in its highest form, with no self-consciousness, just pure "doing it." Consider how a child plays and you will feel what I have in mind. A child fully engaged in play is completely involved and not to be interrupted: This is play felt as serious and total.

It follows from this origin that the greatest reward teaching has to offer is the opportunity to cause this experience to happen again in other, usually younger, people. We teachers want others to feel what we have felt. I have said that what we felt was childlike, but there is more to it than that. We also felt, at the beginning of our experience with English, that we were being initiated into larger worlds, adult worlds, ideas that older people wrote about and cared about. There was a time in our lives when the feelings and situations in *Hamlet* could not move us, but, once they did, there was no going back; we had crossed a threshold and had moved, in some undefinable way, toward adulthood. Thus, if part of what engaged us about our field was a feeling of child-connected delight, another was an intimation of what it means to be an adult; intimations, indeed, of immortality *and* mortality.

The child and the adult, then, are both sources of energy for teaching. Not the child as pupil, note, but the child in the teacher. This is the inner child described in Chapter 2 as the source of good teaching. We look now at the threat that losing that inner child poses to us, and, finally, at the informing myth of the growth of the child's connection to the adult in teaching and in our teaching lives. For it is one thing to understand the importance of the child, but it is quite another to maintain our relationship with it through years, decades, of the work.

For the discouraged or even burned-out teacher, renewal begins with a reconnection to the child-energy. This will come as no revelation at this point. But consider the nature of the child: It is open, non-judgmental, taking in experience "whole," without wondering very much about the norms of the surrounding society. The child, moreover, is open not only to actual experience, but to the numinous, the transpersonal: matters of life, death, eternity, and the bright and dark images and figures that go with them. *Why* and *What if . . .* are two of the great questions of children. They may be put off or puzzled or intimidated by our fumbling answers, but they seldom hesitate to ask the questions unless their parents or teachers are intolerant or uncaring. A child's openness, this willingness to ask, is a prerequisite for actual experience of "otherness." The experience of literature is an extension of this asking, but it is more, because we can lose ourselves in the world of the author. We suspend for a time the ordinary reality of our lives. In the same way a child can become many people: a doctor, a movie star, a cartoon character, a firefighter, a parent. The older we get the harder this becomes, but almost everyone can remember what it was like.

The fact that we do remember shows that there is no distinct separation between the particular child and the universal child. We have all experienced both. We have heard from Guggenbuhl-Craig (1979) on this subject in Chapter 2. Here, again, is his very important basic thesis, followed by his description of the loss of the child-in-the-teacher:

The teacher-student encounter runs parallel to an inner tension between the states of being a knowledgeable adult and an unknowing child. In every adult there is a child who constantly leads us on to new things. The adult's knowledge makes him rigid and inaccessible to innovation. The unknowing child's irrational experimentation, his naive openness, must be retained as a living potential in every adult if he is to remain emotionally alive. Thus the adult is never completely grown up; if he is to be somewhat healthy psychically, he must always keep a certain childlike unknowingness. . . .

One often meets teachers who have lost every trace of childishness, who have even fewer childish traits than the average healthy adult. Such teachers have become "only-teachers," who confront unknowing children almost as their enemy. They complain that children know nothing and do not wish to learn; their nerves are torn by their students' childishness and lack of self-control. For this kind of teacher children are the Other, that which he himself wishes never to be. [His shadow, in other words.] Such teachers derive a certain pleasure from demonstrating their power over children, tormenting them and keeping them in line with carefully calculated mathematical "averages." (104–5)

I will next quote again Guggenbuhl-Craig's central point, but adding now his description of the devastating process which follows the death of the inner child:

The archetype by which the good teacher is fascinated is that of the knowing adult–unknowing child. A good teacher must stimulate the knowing adult in each child, so to speak, just as the doctor must arouse the patient's inner healing factor. But this can only happen if the teacher does not lose touch with his own childishness. In practical terms this means, for example, that he must not lose spontaneity in his teaching and he must let himself be guided somewhat by his own interests. He must not only transmit knowledge but also awaken a thirst for knowledge in the children, but he can only do this if the knowledge-hungry, spontaneous child is still alive within him.

Unfortunately, modern school regimens and teaching plans use every possible means to destroy these spontaneous childlike qualities, for the teaching archetype is split. The teacher's childishness is repressed and then projected on to the pupils. When this happens, learning progress is blocked. The children remain children and the knowing adult is no longer constellated in them. The teacher becomes smarter and the pupils more stupid. Such a teacher, who has split off the childish pole of the archetype, then complains that his pupils used to be so much more eager to learn. His contact with children is made only through power and discipline. At the same time he becomes bitter and saddened. The new, the fresh, the childishly enthusiastic in him has died. Children are his enemies, representing the internally split pole of the archetype, whose reunification is attempted through power. (104–6)

There are two terms in this passage that want amplification: repression and projection. Both of them are unconscious processes, and the thing to remember about the unconscious is that it is unconscious. We can become conscious *of* it by talking about it, but we can't change its nature: We can't make the unconscious conscious. Now to repression. Thoughts and feelings that are too painful to live with are repressed into the unconscious, from whence they come back to us disguised beyond all recognition. They may come back as strong but inexplicable feelings ("I don't know what came over me"). They emerge in dreams as images and unknown people and strange places. Here our concern is that these repressed materials will come back as *projections*. Example: Imagine a husband who, *unconsciously*, fears, or dislikes, or doesn't love his wife—or at least some important aspect of her. How does he describe this situation? In the safety of the local bar, he says to his friend the bartender, "My wife doesn't understand me." And he means it. But what he has done is to project his own inner, unconscious disconnection to his wife on to her. Actually (but unconsciously) he fears or dislikes his own feelings; and, unconsciously, it is himself (and these feelings) that he doesn't understand. So he projects this non-understanding on to his wife. And believe me, he really is convinced of the truth of what he says: To him it really does feel as if she does not understand him. What he says is what he really does feel. But the real truth is not known to him because the unconscious is unconscious. The general principle is that painful feelings are often repressed into the unconscious and then reappear as projections.

So it is in the classroom. As the child in the teacher is repressed into his unconscious, the students come to seem more distant, more ignorant, more uncaring, less worth the effort. Of course it is the child in the teacher that is really disappearing, but that loss is too painful to face, and so the teacher sees the dying as happening outside, in the classroom, rather than as inside, in himself. Rather than honoring the child within, such a teacher will try instead to force adulthood on his students. This is what "reunification through power" means: an attempt to accomplish by force what can only really be done through the establishment of new ties to the inner child. This problem is not a matter of understanding, in an intellectual sense; rather it is a growth of awareness that is needed. Intellect alone will not do it, a fact which makes the process of renewal difficult to describe in rational or discursive language. We know that it is our inner child that makes our students feel like responsible adults. That in turn makes them feel they must help us out. And this is how real education proceeds, as we have already seen. But observing this relationship between child and adult is difficult and subtle. These largest issues in the human psyche have been represented, in all cultures and for all time, in myth. It is therefore to a myth that I now turn.

The example I want to use is the account of Hermes and Apollo we find in the wonderful "Hymn to Hermes" in the *Homeric Hymns* (Boer 1979). At the beginning of the hymn we get a succinct summary of the story of Hermes:

> Born in the morning
> He played the lyre
> by afternoon, and
> by evening had stolen the cattle
> of the archer Apollo. (19)

Here is the child who is at once creative and destructive. On the one hand he invents the lyre by killing a turtle and stringing thongs across the hollow of its shell. On the other hand he not only steals some of Apollo's sacred cattle, but he kills two of them. Apollo, for his part, is both furious and amused; furious because of the theft but amused that such a deed could be carried out by a newborn baby. Hermes denies everything, and Apollo sees that he is up against a formidable trickster:

> And the two of them
> went on discussing
> each of their points in detail,
> the shepherd Hermes
> and the noble son of Leto,
> both of them angry—
> one of them, speaking truthfully
> and not without reason,
> seized glorious Hermes
> for the sake of his cattle—
> the other, the one from Cyllene,
> wanted to deceive Silver-Bow
> with tricks and clever words.
> But even though he was himself
> very shrewd,
> Hermes
> had come up against someone
> very smart. (40)

Even though Apollo is still angry at this point, and even though Hermes is a baby, there is an equality here: The baby feels as able as the adult. It is this equality in position which must obtain between adult and inner child for the adult to be able to feel the child's energy and so be renewed by it.

As the story continues, Hermes and Apollo come to their father Zeus, on Olympus, for final arbitration. Each makes a long speech, but Hermes, after loudly announcing that he is not guilty, *winks* at Zeus. Zeus, laughing at the pure gall of the child, orders the two gods to reconcile themselves to one another. He also orders Hermes to reveal where he has hidden the stolen cattle. The reconciliation is accomplished through the lyre Hermes has made from the turtle's shell. Hermes teaches Apollo how to play it, after he has sung Apollo a song recounting the births of all the immortals. He then gives the lyre to Apollo. Both the song and the gift are important: the song, because it shows that Hermes has knowledge of the common bond that links all the gods, including himself and Apollo; the gift, because the child Hermes must here teach the adult Apollo:

Take this clear-voiced companion
in your hands
and sing—
you know how to express yourself
beautifully and in harmony.
And how swell it is, too,
to bring it
to some rollicking festival,
to some pleasant dance,
even to all-out revelry!
It's fun day or night!
The person who really works at it,
studying it with craft
and intelligence,
who learns to do it pleasantly,
sounding it expertly,
easily entertains
with its pleasures,
driving away
work's weariness.
But if some lunkhead
comes along
and goes at it furiously,
it's hopeless,
every note will be wrong
and struck into the air.
It's up to you
to learn
whatever it is you want.
And I'm even going to give it to you,
noble son of Zeus. (52)

In return, Apollo gives his cattle to Hermes, and the two swear that they will be bonded, in friendship and trust, forever. This is a bond, note, between irrepressible childhood and adult rationality, a bond formed in the process of each coming to know and respect the other's qualities. The child and the adult, then, are seen as equal in power even though different in character and age. Each draws energy from the other: cattle and lyre are exchanged. This myth serves as a paradigm for the process of bringing the child and the adult together as equals, which is exactly what happens, ideally, both within the teacher and in the classroom. What starts as a conflict—with shadow projections going both ways—ends with a pact of mutual support. And Zeus, note, orders them to work it out between themselves: He doesn't do it for them. The process of reconnecting with the child must be this way for us. We have to do it for ourselves. It isn't something that can be mandated from the outside or included in administrative procedures. It is up to us. We must look into our own lives for our own inner child.

Consider again Wordsworth's "Intimations" Ode. In the chapter on Story I described a way of working in our own lives, from Progoff's *Intensive Journal*. Such a procedure is a useful beginning. It "loosens the soil of our lives," as Progoff says, and it lets the child we remember speak to us. Our remembered child is a part of our story, and so we can use it to link ourselves to our students' stories.

But although there will be places where they resemble one another, our remembered child is not the same as the child whose energy we now seek. That energy is in the archetypal foundation of third-stage teaching. And that foundation is in a paradox, a combination of opposites: it is in the *wise child*: ultimately, the *divine child*. We have seen, in Guggenbuhl-Craig, what happens when the teacher's inner child dies, and we have also seen what happens when our students feel the living child in us, and so grow toward the maturity they will need to care for it, and so for us. But the wise child, the divine child, is something else. It is a child, but it does not need to be cared for because it can care for itself; it is a child, yet it knows all there is to know. At the same time its wisdom has not diminished its openness and its excitement. And it is that combination of wisdom and openness that sustains the teacher. For most people openness is gradually replaced, so to speak, by wisdom: The old become oracular and distant, like Zeus. But a life of teaching is not fulfilling if it ends thus. It can only be fulfilling if the joy of the new is as present as the joy of the known.

There is clearly more to Hermes than impulsive fun, as we have seen from the *Homeric Hymns*. Hermes has mastered the lyre (one aspect of public performance, and a good example of a learned skill), and he has also mastered rhetoric: He holds his own in debate with both Apollo (wisdom) and Zeus (power). The great significance of Hermes, for any teacher, is that Hermes stands between the child and the adult, between impulse and skill, between the mortals and the immortals. Specifically, there are three aspects of Hermes that inform teaching: (1) He stands where teachers stand; he stands in *liminal space*; (2) He is a *trickster*, and so knows how to seem unknowing while actually knowing; and (3) he is a *messenger*, a crosser of borders, bringing words from Olympus. And "Olympus," here, holds both the *logos* of ideas and understandings (represented by Apollo) and the *eros* of faith, hope, and love represented by Hera, Demeter, and Aphrodite. Hermes moves between all these realms. Let us look at these three ways of Hermes in the life of teaching.

## LIMINALITY

Liminal space is betwixt and between, literally neither here nor there. The classic studies of liminal space are those of van Gennep (1960). Van Gennep outlined three phases in the rites of passage that mark off one stage of life from the next: rites of separation, rites of liminality, and rites of reincorporation. Turner, following this paradigm, describes liminality:

The neophyte may be buried, forced to lie motionless in the posture and direction of customary burial, may be stained black, or may be forced to live for a while in the company of masked and monstrous mummers representing, *inter alia*, the dead, or, worse, the un-dead. The metaphor of dissolution is often applied to neophytes. . . .

The other aspect, that they are not yet classified, is often expressed in symbols modeled on processes of gestation and parturition. The neophytes are likened to or treated as embryos, newborn infants, or sucklings by symbolic means which vary from culture to culture. . . .

The essential feature of these symbolizations is that the neophytes are neither living nor dead from one aspect, both living and dead from another. Their condition is one of ambiguity and paradox, a confusion of all the customary categories. Liminality may perhaps be regarded as the Nay to all positive structural assertions, but also in some sense the source of them all, and, more than that, a realm of pure possibility whence novel configurations of ideas and new relations may arise. . . .

We are not dealing with structural contradictions when we discuss liminality, but with the essentially unstructured (which is at once destructured and prestructured) and often the people themselves see this in terms of bringing neophytes into close connection with deity and superhuman power. (95–99).

This passage may sound entirely too anthropological. I do not think it is. Specifically, I want to consider the school—and the classroom—as liminal space. One does not have to look very far to find Turner's "ambiguity and paradox" in any school. In most urban high schools, students, no matter what their backgrounds and their lives may be, are nevertheless expected to act like adults. Teachers doing hall duty call out "young man!" or "young lady!" to latecomers, in a mocking tone that suggests this ambiguity exactly: The words are honorific but the tone says that the student is anything but a lady or a man. Often teachers, seeking to quiet down a class, will single out a student and ask, "Sam, why are you talking?" as if Sam *knew* why he was talking and would answer the question; but everyone, Sam included, knows perfectly well that the intent of the teacher is not to ask a question but to quiet the class. Thus an "adult" sort of question is used to achieve what amounts to control over undisciplined children. The liminality here is that the students are seen both ways at once. Expected to act like adults, they are nevertheless treated like children. Here once again is a part of the "hidden curriculum" (Jackson 1968). It is a way schools inculcate the habit of subservience to the general good of the collective society. Naturally students resist this. Since the late 1960's their resistance has taken the form of developing an entirely sufficient and self-perpetuating culture of their own, involving their own music, raps, clothing, language ("he was, like, weird, you know?"), often (alas) gangs, drugs, or criminal behavior. Those who do stay in school (only about half of the total school population) do so often only because they are able to see, in the lives of their successful parents, the long-range payoff of the otherwise irrelevant-seeming initiatory rites of school. For those who cannot see their future in this way, life in the street becomes progressively more real and more attractive as they grow older. *But for neither group is school itself their true reality.* In a wonderful study, (Csikszentmihaly and Larson 1984, 198–217) researchers asked seventy-five students in a large suburban high school to carry electronic pagers for a week at all times, day and night. At one random moment during each twenty-four-hour period each pager was signaled. When it beeped the students were to stop everything and fill out a self-report form describing not only what they were doing when they were beeped but also what they were thinking and feeling. When these students were beeped during class, only 40% of the time was their attention on academic work. And even when it was, they were more often than not apathetic about it, or wishing to be somewhere else (203–4). And that is *during class.* Attention to the academic side of school is practically nonexistent at other times. School, in short, is something to be got through or got out of. In this sense it is liminal, "neither here nor there." In order to cope with this reality it is necessary for a teacher to join her students in shared liminal space.

We have seen our student teacher, Ms. Shepley, do this. When she greeted her small early morning class with her satiric "good morrr-ning," she had brought an element of play, of "kidding," into the room. Consider what she did not do. She did not order the students to be silent. Neither did she say, "All right, it's time to get down to work." She was helped to be the way she was, of course, by her own liminal status as a student, a status in which she is somewhat like her charges in front of her. Experienced teachers have a harder time with this. They feel a need to be more adult, more authoritative. "Don't smile until Christmas" is the often-heard advice from a seasoned veteran. One of the categories in Flanders' Interaction Analysis protocol for describing teacher and student talk is his category one, teacher talk which accepts feeling. As I gathered data for my dissertation I noticed that well over half of all the ones I recorded happened *before the class was officially under way.* A student might say something about the game the team lost on Saturday, and the teacher would commiserate: That's a one. So is a celebration of a bit of good news. But once the class was underway, the ones almost disappeared. It was as if the feelings of students ceased to matter in comparison with what was being taught. And this was true even in discussions of literature.

An awareness of the liminality of school itself cures this. Teaching happens on the border between childhood and adulthood, between unknowing and knowing, between mystery and certainty. Good teachers know how to live in this liminal space: They contain, and therefore express, knowledge and uncertainty at once. For this reason they pick up, intuitively, the pain that comes from uncertainty—the pain that is, for many students, at the very core of their lives. A good teacher can carry this pain. Another side of teachers' liminality is that they deliberately and consciously plan to be something of a mystery to their students; they are always slightly unpredictable, and they enjoy being this way. This is of course the child, which establishes an alliance with students based on a common liminality.

Finally, in connection with liminality, we may ask, Where is the knowledge that the teacher is supposed to convey? Surely knowledge cannot be liminal? Knowledge, it would seem, is facts, things-you-have-to-know. Nothing puzzling or ambiguous about that. But things are not as they seem. It is true of course that teachers are expected to know their subjects. But only people who have not taught think that knowing and teaching are closely connected. For teaching is not the mere transmission of knowledge; if it were, schools could consist entirely of libraries and computer terminals. The fact is that the knowledge with which we as teachers are concerned exists in liminal space.

This becomes immediately clear if we look at the teacher's knowledge from the student's point of view. Everyone has had the experience of sitting in a class and not understanding what the teacher is explaining. This situation is made worse, of course, if some of the other students are understanding what is being taught with seeming ease. The knowledge is seen by the non-understander as *possible* to understand but baffling nevertheless. (I felt this way in mathematics classes year in and year out.) And because we use the metaphor of "progress" for understanding, there is always an implicit connection, in schools, between the mastery of a concept (or a set of facts) and moving along in one's life. Mastery of the binomial theorem now will lead to calculus—a more mature state—down the road. For this reason the knowledge that the teacher has, and that the more gifted students have, comes to represent, for the rest of the students, neither the completely known (obviously it isn't), nor the unknowable, truly adult position. From the students' point of view, the teacher's knowledge represents what has been called a *transitional object* (Winnicott 1974).

Winnicott hypothesizes that the newborn baby (when its mother is "good enough") finds its needs met but, at the very beginning, lives in a world where there is no "outside" mother; rather, the baby's hunger *creates* the breast. The baby's entire reality is its own subjectivity. However, as time passes, the baby's needs are not always optimally met, and it finds substitute objects (its own thumb, for one) which exist in an "intermediate area" between inner subjective reality and objective reality, which is outer and other. The thumb, then the blanket, then the teddy bear, exist in this liminality. He writes:

My claim is . . . [that] the third part of the life of a human being, a part that we cannot ignore, is an intermediate area of *experiencing*, to which inner reality and external life both contribute. . . .

I am here staking a claim, for an intermediate state between a baby's inability and his growing ability to recognize and accept reality. I am therefore studying the substance of *illusion*, that which is allowed to the infant, and which in adult life is inherent in art and religion. (3)

We can imagine the teacher's knowledge in this way because it seems to the student to be neither objectively "out in the world" *nor* subjectively owned by him—contained, so to speak, in his own mind. It is out there but not yet owned. Learning does not proceed in a linear way from ignorance to explanation to understanding, except at the lowest levels of instruction, such as the directions for assembling a lawn chair. Rather, what happens is that the student (1) is puzzled by something completely novel; (2) notices, or has pointed out to her, something familiar within the novel occurrence; (3) looks for other points of familiarity so as to feel more secure with the new idea; (4) finds at some point that the new idea ceases to be a new idea at all. Its liminality has ended. This is another description of a student being moved through Vygotsky's Zone of Proximal Development (see note to Chapter 4).

Most young people, for example, by the time they have reached seventh grade, have learned that "a sentence is a group of words containing a subject and a predicate and expressing a complete thought." If I write on the blackboard *I had corn flakes for breakfast this morning* students will be amused by the banality but they will accept it as a sentence. If I press them they will tell me it's a sentence because it expresses a complete thought. But now, if I write *I had rattlesnake meat for breakfast this morning* seventh graders immediately want to know why I did that, where I had breakfast, what's wrong with me anyway, and so on. Clearly this is a sentence and yet it is anything but a complete thought. And if we discuss this contradiction we will conclude—I hope—that the problem is not in the idea of a sentence (a sentence is recognizable as a sentence no matter what it says) but, rather, in the definition. Thus we are on our way to an important idea: that the descriptions we've learned—called "grammar"—aren't really any good for anything. We must have learned to make, and recognize, sentences in some other way. The question of how we really produce sentences is, of course, at the heart of modern linguistic inquiry. And these students have begun to learn that the old system they've learned doesn't help. They have had to know the old system, for school, but they haven't ever used it for anything other than tests. So for them an old idea of how language works is fading, and a new one hasn't yet taken its place. Eventually they will learn to have both the old and the new available, though, because the public, and parents, still believe in the "old" grammar. If the mark of an educated person is the ability to hold two ideas in one's mind at the same time, then these students are on their way toward achieving the status of being educated people.

The central point here is this: A successful teacher imagines knowledge as being in liminal space. In the end this means that the teacher must always face the question, not *what* do I know, but rather, *how* did I come to know it. I have provided one example of this by tracing the history of my reading of Cather's "Paul's Case." For me to teach that story successfully I need to remain mindful of the fact that the story still scares me irrationally; that is, it still is in liminal space for me. Only those things which we do not completely understand ourselves will fully engage us when we teach them. "Not understanding" means that we are in liminal space, with the subject—the story, the poem, the principle of linguistics—staying somewhat unknown. In other words, the subject itself will feel liminal to us. And, because our students are already in liminal space by virtue of their age, it is only when we, too, enter liminal space that will we be truly teaching. It is the one place where we can meet up with them.

## THE TRICKSTER

Here is an example of a basic concept (number and numeral) as taught by the trickster.

The difference between *number* (a property of objects, of the physical world: two pencils, eighteen thousand Chicago Bulls fans), and *numeral* (an arbitrary symbol used to represent the property of number: 2, 18,000) is a fundamental concept in mathematics. It is a concept that is hard for students, though, because most of their early experience with numerals is blurred, in school, with experiences or descriptions containing a number: "If George has three pencils and Sally has two, how many . . . ?" and so on. This confuses young children because they persist in imagining pencils, not numerals, even though the teacher's covert agenda (the shadow of power again) is to teach techniques for manipulating numerals.

Imagine now a teacher of mathematics who wants to make her seventh grade class really aware of the number/numeral distinction. She has many choices to make about how to do this. She could, of course, explain the concept, pretty much as I have just done. That is the way school usually proceeds, alas.

Now imagine another way. The class arrives in its usual chaotic, that is, seventh-grade, way, and settles down, more or less. The teacher watches but says nothing. This silence on the part of the teacher is a bit unusual, and so now, because nothing is happening, the students become a bit more watchful. Still saying nothing, she walks over to the board and, using the whole length of her piece of chalk sideways, she writes a huge 5. "Do you see this?" she asks; her students are entertained by the absurdity of her question. Of course they can see it. "All right," she says. "Now *watch*. And get ready for a question." She goes back to the board and, near the giant 5, she writes a tiny, barely legible *100*. "Are you

ready for the question?" "Yes!" "All right, here's the question."
She waits until the room is absolutely silent. "Here's the question:
*Which one is larger?*"

The resulting discussion should be one of those that engenders
the true joy that teaching can bring. The "number" people will
choose the 5; those who see numerals will choose the 100. Both are
right. Both are wrong. It is a pure delight, this lesson. And it will
make its point. (Eventually, of course, the class will see that both
ideas are true; another instance of understanding moving out of
the liminal and into the known.)

In English there is an equivalent lesson. Draw a picture of a
house on the board. Ask the class to "take out a piece of scratch
paper and write down what that is." Almost everyone will write
down *house*. Ask one who has done so to come up to the board and
open the door. Students will then correct their answers to something like "a picture of a house." Then erase the picture, write the
*word* "HOUSE," and ask where the connection is between the
word, the picture, and the thing. "In the head," someone will
eventually say. By this route the class will come to know the
Ogden-Richards model of symbol, concept, and referent; more
generally, how language stands in relation to reality. There is
nothing especially innovative about such teaching: It was all the
rage in the sixties, when "discovery learning" was a cornerstone
of the new mathematics and science curricula then being developed. It still is compelling. What is important for our purpose here
is that the teacher has deliberately disrupted the ordinary logic of
the classroom. Students have been fooled, but for the purpose of
engaging them: The trick tricks them into thinking.

Leon Festinger (1957) held the theory that the human mind is
by its nature interested only in those experiences which are new to
it. Once it has experienced something and come to "understand"
it, it will not willingly return to this known ground. If Festinger is
right—and I think he is—then part of a teacher's task is to be the
trickster. The trickster sets up things in such a way that people are
caught in their own habitual ways and made to feel exposed,
foolish, or outsmarted. That would be cruel if no good came of it.
But there is good in the work of the trickster. The trickster *sets up
problems so that they can be resolved*. He is a troublemaker in a good
cause.

We have seen Hermes at this. Stealing the cattle of Apollo is upsetting to Apollo precisely because Apollo's world by itself has no unexpectedness in it at all. Apollo is the god of moderation, of reason, of cool intellect. As are all the gods (except Hermes), Apollo is one-sided. He *needs* to be unsettled now and again.

Schools are one-sided in the same way that Apollo is. For this reason the Hermetic teacher sees surprise, the unexpected, the "discrepant" event (Festinger's term) as necessary elements in the classroom. Such things not only get attention. They also make for an atmosphere in which another aspect of the liminal is brought into play. I mean the boundary between order and chaos. This is really the same as the boundary between the known and the unknown. As Lopez-Pedraza says, "Hermes, 'Lord of the Roads' as he came to be known, also marks our psychological roads and boundaries; he marks the borderlines of our psychological frontiers and marks the territory where, in our psyche, the foreign, the alien, begins" (1989, 14). This border is where our students live. If school is overly orderly and "known" it will seem to our students to be stultifyingly artificial and disconnected from their experience. But if school is chaotic it will be meaningless: The trick (the trickster's task) is to stay on this boundary (liminality again). Hermes in our story steals the cattle (chaos) but invents and masters the lyre (order). Teachers, too, must do both.

## THE MESSENGER

Lopez-Pedraza writes,

Hermes is known as the messenger of the gods; in other words, mythologically, he connects the gods and goddesses to each other and to man. . . . [L]et us imagine Hermes touching those spots where we are most sorely afflicted, thereby connecting to them and, at the same time, connecting us to them. As the connection-maker, he gives us a new view of an episode in our lives, or of a pathology. . . . At the same time he reveals the psychic value in what has not seemed to be relevant or was hidden. In this way, Hermes is a god of transformation. (8)

This seems obvious enough, but there is a profound significance in this passage. Consider, from a *student's* point of view, what it means to gain "a new view of an episode" in his, or her, life. This would mean no less than a shift in that student's idea of how things are, and this in turn mean a shift in the student's idea of his or her identity. This is a fundamentally important experience, especially for an adolescent. Adolescents in general feel themselves to be trapped between a greater and a nether millstone. The greater millstone is how the adult world is *said* (by teachers and parents) to work; the nether millstone is how they themselves *know* it to work. It is no wonder that teachers and parents alike experience their adolescent charges as overly self-assured, cocky, and brash one minute and vacillating, withdrawn, and hesitant the next. They are oscillating between the world as it has been made for them and the world which they are trying to make for themselves. Often they feel that they will grow into adulthood just by mastering a technique. The driver's license is a talisman for one such technique. So is the use of drugs or alcohol. So is sexual activity, or pregnancy. It is easy enough for us wise adults to see through these emblems of adulthood, but for our students they have genuine adult validity. Or, more accurately, students are sure they have such validity. Is there anything we, as teachers, might do to be a messenger who tells such students something about what growing to adulthood is really about? Or must we passively wait for them to do it on their own?

Note that the issue here is not what the message should be: That is easy. Anyone can *tell* someone else a message. The issue is more subtle: It is how to *be a messenger*. Hermes doesn't just carry messages; he embodies the message himself. Therefore he is, in a word, *effective*. He speaks, as Homer says, "in winged words." Translated over into teaching, he establishes the sort of connection that excellent teachers seem to have with their pupils. These are the teachers who are remembered years afterward; not necessarily with love, but at least with awe mixed with some measure of affection. They are remembered because they have done something somewhere within the student's psyche. My hypothesis is that they have successfully touched what Lopez-Pedraza calls "an afflicted spot." Where the student felt pain, puzzlement, frustration—a deep unknowing, too deep to be acknowledged—the teacher brought healing. Order, method, and peace were substituted for chaos and uncertainty and hurt. How does this happen?

For one thing, I believe such teachers have never lost sight of what they received from *their* teachers. They have remained full of gratitude for the healing they received. I do not believe anyone can successfully teach who has not been successfully taught. It may be, in some instances, that they have taught themselves, as Thoreau did at Walden Pond. But even here there has to have been a purpose clearly in mind: "I wanted to front the essential facts" Thoreau said, of his withdrawal from ordinary collective life. And there must be gratitude for the experience. Hermes' first act, after birth, is to sing a hymn of praise to his father and mother, not just because they had him, but because he is delighted to celebrate who they are—Zeus and Maia. Hermes knows his lineage and is happy with it. Lineage is a key to good teaching: How we teach is not just made up on the spot. It is a reflection of how we were taught, and how we were taught is derived from how our teachers were taught, and so on. And this history extends back, generation by generation. Even the gods can be taught, as Hermes shows Apollo. So teachers bring not only knowledge of a particular subject to the classroom. They bring with them the whole history of the conveyance, from one generation to the next, of all that is known and valued.

This idea is seldom celebrated in the teachers' lounge. And it often comes up negatively in the classroom: "You'll have to know this for the test" is just a pale mimicry of "You'll have to know this for your life." Here the teacher knows, or rather purports to know, what it is necessary to know later. This is another manifestation of the shadow of the teacher, expressed in the form of a threat to students. The atmosphere of threat, thus created, guarantees that the message, no matter if valid, will not be heard.

As we have seen, though, the message will be heard if students feel they have to care for the teacher's child; it will be heard if it resonates with something already in the student; it is more likely to be heard if the shadowy need for power has been worked through by the teacher. More generally, the message will be heard if teacher and student are together accepting of liminality. And up to this point, I have tried to make as strong a case as I can for teachers to stay in liminal space, suspended between unknowing and knowing, containing in one person both the child and the adult in mutual coexistence and conflict at once. It is this tension—

this excitement—that drives teachers into the third stage and that keeps them there.

A professional lifetime dependent on liminality, the trickster, and knowledge understood as transitional rather than unknown or known is a lifetime lived on the edge. Every day, every class, every encounter with a student, will have the quality of a conflict of opposites with a mystery between them. It is the quality of Hermes to live in this mystery, even to thrive on it. It is his nature. But Hermes is a god, an immortal. The gods and goddesses live in their various natures untroubled by all other ways of being, and they exist in their individually defined ways eternally. Not so for us ordinary mortals. We grow older. Our natures change. To advocate the teacher as Hermes is to advocate a state—Carlsen's third stage—which, once entered into, is to be maintained *unchanged* for all our years of teaching. And it is an edgy, nervous, energy-draining, risky stage at that. Delightful and exhilarating as this stage is, it cannot be maintained year after year. We cannot go on forever stealing cattle, inventing musical instruments, lying shamelessly to our elders and then making up with them. We cannot forever cross borders and carry messages. All this is "rough magic." So in my final chapter I propose a fourth stage. If the third stage is a tension between the opposites of child and adult, a stage lived in liminality, the fourth stage is a resolution of that tension, a movement to a unitary state in which the final triumph of the teacher is that, paradoxically, he becomes unnecessary. It is a sea change, an extinction of personality. The exemplar is no longer Hermes. But Hermes has taken us far, and it is worthwhile to look back in gratitude before moving on. But move on we shall. The figure who represents this fourth and final stage is Shakespeare's Prospero. We turn, in the final chapter, to him and his world.

## WORKS CITED

Boer, Charles. *The Homeric Hymns*. Dallas: Spring Publications, 1979.

Csikszentmihaly, Mihaly, and Reed Larson. *Being Adolescent*. New York: Basic Books, 1984.

Emig, Janet. "Non-Magical Thinking: Presenting Writing Developmentally in High Schools." In *The Web of Meaning*. Upper Montclair, New Jersey: Boynton-Cook, 1983

Festinger, Leon. *A Theory of Cognitive Dissonance*. Palo Alto, California: Stanford University Press, 1957.

Guggenbuhl-Craig, Adolf. *Power in the Helping Professions*. Dallas: Spring Publications, 1979.

Jackson, Philip. *Life in Classrooms*. New York: Holt, Rinehart and Winston, 1968.

Lopez-Pedraza, Rafael. *Hermes and His Children*. Einsiedeln, Switzerland: Daimon Verlag, 1989.

Sanford, John. *Ministry Burnout*. New York: Paulist Press, 1982.

Turner, V. W. *The Forest of Symbols: Aspects of Ndembu Ritual*. Ithaca and London: Cornell University Press, 1967.

van Gennep, A. *The Rites of Passage*. Chicago: The University of Chicago Press, 1960.

Winnicott, D. W. *Playing and Reality*. New York: Penguin, 1974.

*Chapter Seven*

# Rough Magic Abjured: Freedom and Letting Go

*Prospero*:  I have bedimmed
The noontide sun, called forth the mutinous winds . . .
But this rough magic
I here abjure.

—*The Tempest*, Act 5, Scene 1

At the end of the eleven weeks of her student teaching, Ms. Shepley could look back with a good deal of satisfaction. She is right to do so; she has come far. Problems of control and pacing that seemed insurmountable have ceased to exist at all: She simply knows what to do. Students who once scared her she now holds in affectionate regard. Indeed she returned to her school some weeks after she'd finished her teaching. She just wanted to visit with her cooperating teacher and the department head, but, as she made her way to the English office, former students spotted her and ran up to her, urging her to return, to teach them some more. She wasn't expecting such a welcome, and she was moved and encouraged by it.

And this is the usual pattern, happily, for most student teachers: They begin with fear and uncertainty, and they are exhausted by the fact that, no matter how little time they have to prepare for it, the next day will bring the same crowds of students and the same seemingly impossible demands. And the next day this will be just as true—and the next. Nevertheless they gradually master enough of the craft so that, at the end, they look back at how they were and wonder at how far they have come. Watching this process has been, for me, the greatest reward of directing a teacher education program. Such students are ready to embark; that is, they are ready to try to move through the three stages of a teaching life, with the culminating third stage being their expression of their true selves through what they do, day in and day out, in their teaching. To reach that stage is a rich reward.

But if the third stage is endlessly rewarding, it is endlessly demanding too. It is demanding of time and energy because it involves the tension of opposites held together: child and adult, liminal space, the trickster controlled just enough, knowledge treated as unknown. Some people—I do not think very many— can maintain this level of accomplishment for a lifetime of teaching. They remain, in an admirable way, the center of their own attention. It is attention focused on what this book has been about so far: the mastery of craft and the sustaining of energy for the work through a connection with its archetypal core. But I believe there is a fourth stage in a teaching life, a stage beyond the three which Carlsen so trenchantly describes. If our attention stays on the teacher this fourth stage will be hard, or impossible, to see. To see it we must look instead at the student.

For many years I was sustained, and moved, by students who would cluster around me after class was dismissed on the last day of school and tell me how much they had enjoyed what we'd done, and how much they wished they could have me again next year. Tears, on both sides, were sometimes a part of these scenes. (Those tears, of course, made it harder to see the students who just hurried along to their next class.) But I now know that such an ending, with its "Goodbye, Mr. Chips" overtones, is not truly a mark of what good teaching is all about.

I want to suggest that the *ultimate* sign of successful teaching is a sequence that plays out this way: First, a student is puzzled, even upset, by a discrepancy, a painful occurrence in a story, a concept not understood. But the teaching proceeds; the student listens, talks, writes. The problem comes up again, in a slightly different form. The student works at it some more. But then, at a certain point—as in my earlier example of the "sentence" definition—the student *owns* the new idea. At that moment it ceases to be new. In fact, if the new idea is inherently true to the student's nature, true to human nature in general, then the newness will disappear insensibly into familiarity. At this point the student may very well say, with a certain wonderment: "I knew that. I knew that, all along."

*For the student to feel this is the goal of teaching.* If the student feels gratitude then there is still a dependency, however beneficent. For the shadow of gratitude is the need for more. The shadow, the dark brother, of gratitude, is greed, and if I think I can forever feed the greedy student then I am inflated: I am not a teacher but an oracle.

This final stage, then, happens *in the student.* For this reason we have come to the end of the power vested in techniques (or "methods") of teaching; we have come to the end, even, of the heuristic value in the Hermetic archetypal theory on which we have depended so far. Hermes, for all his magical, mercurial qualities, is a technician, a doer. He moves us through the first three stages. For the fourth, we must attend to the art of letting go, the art, not of *conferring* freedom on the student (for that would be to remain in control of it), but rather the art of celebrating the final and total disconnection of student from teacher. An almost perfect paradigm for this letting go is Shakespeare's Prospero.

At the beginning of *The Tempest* a shipwreck, magically orchestrated by Prospero, brings to his island a group of people from the mainland. One is a virtuous elder (Gonzalo) and one is a dependent son (Ferdinand), but most have plotted against Prospero when he was Duke of Milan. Most, in other words, have fallen prey to ambition, greed, and the seductive lure of political position. They are in various states of psychic disrepair. Prospero, through his spirit-agent Ariel, will, during the course of the play, *teach* these people. In the end they will find that they know their true natures. They will be truly free—of the island, of Prospero, and of the false gods (Jungians would say *complexes*) which have possessed them.

For most of the play, Prospero works on them Hermetically, by the means which we have seen. He is a shaman, a messenger from the gods, with Ariel (the child-like spirit, sometimes eager, some-

times moody, but motivated always by the promise of freedom)
doing the work. For most of the play the Prospero/Ariel combination reflects our image of the child-in-the-teacher. But in the end
he gives it all up, knowingly, because his foes, and Ferdinand
(now in love with Prospero's daughter Miranda) have all come to
know themselves. Only Caliban, shadow, remains unchanged. (As
shadow must, being the necessary other that makes all consciousness possible. No light without dark, no good without evil: the
point of the fall in Eden.)

At the very moment when his spell holds all in thrall to him,
Prospero *lets go*:

*Prospero*:          Say, my spirit,
How fares the King and's followers?

*Ariel*:               Confined together
In the same fashion as you gave in charge,
Just as you left them; all prisoners, sir,
In the lime-grove which weather-fends your cell.
They cannot budge till your release. The King,
His brother, and yours, abide all three distracted,
And the remainder mourning over them,
Brimful of sorrow and dismay; but chiefly
Him that you termed, sir, the good old lord Gonzalo,
His tears run down his beard like winter's drops
From eaves of reeds. Your charm so strongly works 'em
That if you now beheld them your affections
Would become tender.

*Prospero*:     Dost thou think so, spirit?

*Ariel*:     Mine would, sir, were I human.

*Prospero*:          And mine shall.
Hast though, which art but air, a touch, a feeling
Of their afflictions, and shall not myself,
One of their kind, that relish all as sharply
Passion as they, be kindlier moved than thou art?
Though with their high wrongs I am struck to th' quick,
Yet with my nobler reason 'gainst my fury
Do I take part. The rarer action is
In virtue than in vengeance. . . .
     Go release them, Ariel.
My charms I'll break, their senses I'll restore,
And they shall be themselves.

*Ariel:*          I'll fetch them, sir.

*Prospero:*   Ye elves of hills, brooks, standing lakes and groves,
          And ye that on the sand with printless foot
          Do chase the ebbing Neptune, and do fly him
          When he comes back; you demi-puppets that
          By moonshine do the green sour ringlets make
          Whereof the ewe not bites; and you whose pastime
          Is to make midnight mushrooms, that rejoice
          To hear the solemn curfew; by whose aid,
          Weak masters though you be, I have bedimmed
          The noontide sun, called forth the mutinous winds,
          And 'twixt the green sea and the azured vault
          Set roaring war—to the dread rattling thunder
          Have I given fire, and rifted Jove's stout oak
          With his own bolt; the strong-based promontory
          Have I made shake, and by the spurs plucked up
          The pine and cedar; graves at my command
          Have waked their sleepers, oped, and let 'em forth
          By my so potent art. But this rough magic
          I here abjure. And when I have required
          Some heavenly music—which even now I do—
          To work mine end upon their senses that
          This airy charm is for, I'll break my staff,
          Bury it certain fathoms in the earth,
          And deeper than did ever plummet sound
          I'll drown my book.

                                   —*The Tempest*, Act 5, Scene 1

Imagine, if you will, Prospero's island as a school. Students, of course, do not bring to school the sophisticated malfeasance that characterizes Prospero's enemies. Some, alas, do bring a fascination with, or an involvement with the criminal, to be sure. But the majority bring, as their fault, simply youth itself, and its accompanying ignorance and distortions. Imagine the classroom as Prospero's island, with the teacher as Prospero. In this imagining, then, in this view of the final stage of a teaching life, the end result will be that the students are somehow "transformed toward maturity" without their ever having known what happened or how it was done. The attachment to the teacher broken, they move on. This is the final achievement of teaching. It is where we move from looking at teaching as a craft to seeing it as an art. Teaching is no longer an expression of the teacher's being; rather, it becomes an expression of the inner adult now alive within the student, empowering that student in magical but insensible ways.

I have said that this is the result of the *art* of teaching. T. S. Eliot, describing the process by which poetry (in his view) is created, describes also a giving up. In his essay "Tradition and the Individual Talent" he writes:

What happens is a continual surrender of himself as he is at the moment to something which is more valuable. The progress of an artist is a continual self-sacrifice, a continual extinction of personality. There remains to define this process of depersonalization . . . the mind of the mature poet differs from the immature one not precisely in any valuation of "personality," not being necessarily more interesting, or having "more to say," but rather in being a more finely perfected medium in which special, or very varied, feelings are at liberty to enter into new combinations . . . the more perfect the artist, the more completely separate in him will be the man who suffers and the mind which creates. . . . The poet's mind is in fact a receptacle for seizing and storing up numberless feelings, phrases, images, which remain there until all the particles which can unite to form a new compound are present together. (7–8)

Robert Frost, in his preface to the 1939 edition of his *Collected Poems*, expresses Eliot's idea in another way. He writes that, for him, a poem succeeds when, in the writing of it, he discovers "something I didn't know I knew" (ix).

What a teacher does is to arrange things so that this process, which feels to the student like a process of discovery but is actually one of *re*covery, of seeing clearly what was previously seen only dimly or not at all, occurs within each student over a period of time. This is especially true in the teaching of English, because literature and language contain the very ground of our being: English is almost always about what is already there. Once this becomes the center of a teacher's attention, all the issues of shadow, of power, disappear, because the teacher is no longer causing knowledge to be transmitted, but is rather enabling its recovery by the student.

This means that in this last stage of teaching, with all the Hermetic technique mastered, and the subject matter sufficiently understood, the teacher's attention shifts from herself to her students. The teacher becomes an advocate for, and a revealer of, their true natures, as they exist both actually and in potential. This attention to the student is usually urged upon beginning teachers too soon. It is common for the supervising teacher to call beginners' attention to a student who is inattentive or puzzled. The fact is that these things will take care of themselves as technique is mastered. But the kind of attention I am advocating here is paradoxical: It is attention to what is already in the student, but at a deep level, at the level of the archetypal ground, which is our *shared* being. At a practical level this means that planning begins with the question, What is already in the student which I can bring forth? In my discussion of "Paul's Case" I indicated that one way to work this way is to begin with the question of what is in one's self. But experience, and attentive reading of student writing, lets us imagine the inner world of our students. Mina Shaughnessy's book *Errors and Expectations* (1971) shows how this can be done with truly disadvantaged writers. We have to live, for a time, in our student's imaginal space, as best we can. Nothing more can be asked of a teacher than this. This is not a technique. It is a way of life, a way of being.

What, then, finally, is the reward? It is the continual presence of *imaginal youth* in the teacher, no matter what the outer vicissitudes of her life may hold. This is the boon that the good teacher, as hero, brings back. For this youth is an elixir for all who come in contact with it. Willa Cather, in *Death Comes for the Archbishop*, portrays this discovery through the aged archbishop. His life is coming to a close, and yet:

In New Mexico he always awoke a young man; not until he rose and began to shave did he realize that he was growing older. His first consciousness was a sense of the light dry wind blowing in through the windows, with a fragrance of hot sun and sage-brush and sweet clover; a wind that made one's body feel light and one's heart cry "To-day, to-day," like a child's.

Beautiful surroundings, the society of learned men, the charm of noble women, the graces of art, could not make up for him the loss of those light-hearted mornings of the desert, for the wind that made one a boy again. He had noticed that this peculiar quality in the air of new countries vanished after they were tamed by man and made to bear harvests. Parts of Texas and Kansas that he had first known as open range had since been made into rich farming districts, and the air had quite lost that lightness, that dry aromatic odour. The moisture of plowed land, the heaviness of labour and growth and grain-bearing, utterly destroyed it; one could breathe that only on the bright edge of the world, on the great grass plains or the sage-brush desert.

That air would disappear from the whole earth in time, perhaps; but long after his day. He did not know just when it had become so necessary to him, but he had come back to die in exile for the sake of it. Something soft and wild and free, something that whispered to the ear on the pillow, lightened the heart, softly, softly picked the lock, slid the bolts, and released the prisoned spirit of man into the wind, into the blue and gold, into the morning, into the morning! (275–76)

The morning of teaching is each new class, each new student. We know, and do not know, what each will bring. But we may be sure that the end of the work comes when the younger or more unknowing people it has been our privilege to guide for a time move away from us, and into the morning of their own understanding and their own sense of themselves. It is this that gives value to the work, and so to the life, of teaching. This is where the example of Prospero is not quite perfect. Prospero, abandoned on his island, spends years studying his art, and his craft, for the sole purpose of teaching one magical, all-encompassing lesson. He does it perfectly. But a teacher's life is not like that. A teacher teaches hundreds, thousands, of lessons in a lifetime. To do this, to be *able* to do this, a teacher must, I believe, breathe the air so celebrated by Cather's archbishop. There a person at the end of a long life feels the boy, the child, still in him. That is the real reward of a life in teaching. Long after there are no more classes, no more schedules—even completely alone—the teacher can see a further reach, a place, an idea, still new. For one having been so long in liminal space, the more assured, more settled ordinary world feels stale, flat, and unprofitable by comparison. The gift teaching gives is a continual experience of the not-yet-known—even the un-knowable—in our students, and in ourselves.

## WORKS CITED

Cather, Willa. *Death Comes for the Archbishop*. New York: Vintage Books, Random House, 1971.

————. *The Troll Garden*. Ed. James Woodress. Lincoln: The University of Nebraska Press, 1983.

Eliot, T. S. *Selected Essays*. New York: Harcourt, Brace and Company, 1950.

Frost, Robert. *Collected Poems*. New York: Henry Holt and Company, 1939.

Shakespeare, William. *The Tempest*. Ed. Northrop Frye. Baltimore: Penguin Books, 1959.

Shaughnessy, Mina. *Errors and Expectations*. New York: Oxford University Press, 1971.

# References

Amidon, Edmund J., and Ned A. Flanders, *The Role of the Teacher in the Classroom*. Minneapolis, Minnesota: Association for Productive Teaching, Inc., 1967.

Boer, Charles. *The Homeric Hymns*. Dallas: Spring Publications, 1979.

Bruner, Jerome S. *The Process of Education*. Cambridge, Massachusetts: Harvard University Press, 1960.

———. *Actual Minds, Possible Worlds*. Cambridge, Massachusetts: Harvard University Press, 1986.

Campbell, Joseph. *The Hero with a Thousand Faces*. Princeton, New Jersey: Princeton University Press, 1949.

Cather, Willa. *Death Comes for the Archbishop*. New York: Vintage Books, Random House, 1971.

———. *The Troll Garden*. Ed. James Woodress. Lincoln: The University of Nebraska Press, 1983.

Csikszentmihaly, Mihaly, and Reed Larson. *Being Adolescent*. New York: Basic Books, 1984.

Eliot, T. S. *The Four Quartets*. New York: Harcourt, Brace and Company, 1943.

———. *Selected Essays*. New York: Harcourt, Brace and Company, 1950.

Ellenberger, Henri F. *The Discovery of the Unconscious*. New York: Basic Books, 1970.

Emig, Janet. "Non-Magical Thinking: Presenting Writing Developmentally in High Schools." In *The Web of Meaning*. Upper Montclair, New Jersey: Boynton-Cook, 1983.

*English Journal*. "Editorial Comment," 78, No. 6, October 1989, 56.

Ferguson, Marilyn. *The Holographic Paradigm*. Ed. Ken Wilbur. Boulder, Colorado: Shambhala Press, 1982.

Festinger, Leon. *A Theory of Cognitive Dissonance*. Palo Alto, California: Stanford University Press, 1957.

Flanders, Ned A. *Analyzing Teacher Behavior*. Palo Alto, California: Addison-Wesley, 1970.

Frost, Robert. *Collected Poems*. New York: Henry Holt and Company, 1939.

Gage, Nathan, ed. *Handbook of Research on Teaching*. Chicago: Rand McNally, 1968.

Guggenbuhl-Craig, Adolf. *Power in the Helping Professions*. Dallas: Spring Publications, 1979.

Guilford, J. P. "The Three Faces of Intellect." *American Psychologist* (1959): 469–79.

Hayakawa, S. I. *Language in Thought and Action*. New York: Harcourt Brace Jovanovich, 1972.

Herndon, James. *The Way It Spozed To Be*. New York: Bantam Books, 1969.

Jackson, Philip. *Life in Classrooms*. New York: Holt, Rinehart and Winston, 1968.

Jung, C. G. "The Development of Personality." *The Development of Personality*. Vol. 17 of *The Collected Works of C. G. Jung*. 20 vols. Princeton, New Jersey: Bollingen Series XX, Princeton University Press, 1954.

———. *Symbols of Transformation*. Vol. 5 of *The Collected Works of C. G. Jung*. 20 vols. Princeton, New Jersey: Bollingen Series XX, Princeton University Press, 1956.

———. *Memories, Dreams, Reflections*. New York: Pantheon Books, 1961.

———. "Answer to Job." *Psychology and Religion: East and West*. Vol. 11 of *The Collected Works of C. G. Jung*. 20 vols. Princeton, New Jersey: Bollingen Series XX, Princeton University Press, 1969.

———. *Freud and Psychoanalysis*. Vol. 4 of *The Collected Works of C. G. Jung*. 20 vols. Princeton, New Jersey: Bollingen Series XX, Princeton University Press, 1970.

———. *Psychological Types*. Vol. 6 of *The Collected Works of C. G. Jung*, 20 vols. Princeton, New Jersey: Bollingen Series XX, Princeton University Press, 1971.

———. "The Psychology of the Transference." *The Practice of Psychotherapy*. Vol. 16 of *The Collected Works of C. G. Jung*. 20 vols.

Princeton, New Jersey: Bollingen Series XX. Princeton University Press, 1977.

Kitzhaber, Albert R. *The Oregon Curriculum, A Sequential Program in English: Literature I.* New York: Holt, Rinehart and Winston, 1967.

Lindley, Daniel A., Jr. "Rhetorical Analysis of Teaching in Selected English Classrooms." Ph.D. Diss. Florida State University, 1970.

———. "The Source of Good Teaching." *English Education* 19 (1987): 159–70.

Lopez-Pedraza, Rafael. *Hermes and His Children.* Einsiedeln, Switzerland: Daimon Verlag, 1989.

McClelland, David C., et al. *The Achieving Society.* New York: Appleton-Century-Crofts, 1953.

Meyers, Isabel Briggs. *Gifts Differing.* Palo Alto, California: Consulting Psychologists Press, 1980.

Progoff, Ira. *At a Journal Workshop.* New York: Dialogue House Library, 1975.

Rodman, F. Robert. *Keeping Hope Alive.* New York: Harper and Row, 1986.

Rosowski, Susan J. *The Voyage Perilous.* Lincoln: The University of Nebraska Press, 1986.

Sanford, John. *Ministry Burnout.* New York: Paulist Press, 1982.

Schwartz, Tony. *The Responsive Chord.* New York: Doubleday, Anchor Press, 1974.

Schwartz-Salant, Nathan. *The Borderline Personality in Analysis: Vision and Healing.* Wilmette, Illinois: Chiron Press, 1989.

Shakespeare, William. *The Tempest.* Ed. Northrop Frye. Baltimore: Penguin Books, 1959.

Shaughnessy, Mina. *Errors and Expectations.* New York: Oxford University Press, 1971.

Tennyson, Alfred Lord. *The Poems and Plays of Alfred Lord Tennyson.* New York: Random House, 1938.

Turner, V. W. *The Forest of Symbols: Aspects of Ndembu Ritual.* Ithaca and London: Cornell University Press, 1967.

U. S. Office of Education, Bureau of Research. *Final Report, Project No. H-026: The Development and Testing of Approaches to the Teaching of English in the Junior High School.* Tallahassee: Florida State University, 1968.

van Gennep, A. *The Rites of Passage.* Chicago: The University of Chicago Press, 1960.

Winnicott, D. W. *Playing and Reality.* New York: Penguin, 1974.

Wordsworth, William. *William Wordsworth: An Illustrated Selection.* Ed. Jonathan Wordsworth. Grasmere, Cumbria: The Wordsworth Trust, 1987.

# Index

**About the Author**

DANIEL A. LINDLEY was for twenty years Associate Professor of English and chair of English Education, University of Illinois at Chicago, after teaching at Yale and Dartmouth. His secondary school teaching was done at the Groton School and the laboratory schools of the University of Illinois, the University of Chicago, and Florida State University. Lindley is a psychotherapist in private practice and is completing the analyst training program of the Jung Institute in Chicago.

## About the Author